Writing Successful Reports and Dissertations

SAGE Study Skills

Writing Successful Reports and Dissertations

Lucinda Becker

SAGE

Los Angeles | London | New Delhi
Singapore | Washington DC

Los Angeles | London | New Delhi
Singapore | Washington DC

SAGE Publications Ltd
1 Oliver's Yard
55 City Road
London EC1Y 1SP

SAGE Publications Inc.
2455 Teller Road
Thousand Oaks, California 91320

SAGE Publications India Pvt Ltd
B 1/I 1 Mohan Cooperative Industrial Area
Mathura Road
New Delhi 110 044

SAGE Publications Asia-Pacific Pte Ltd
3 Church Street
#10-04 Samsung Hub
Singapore 049483

Editor: Katie Metzler
Assistant editor: Lily Mehrbod
Production editor: Ian Antcliff
Copyeditor: Sarah Bury
Proofreader: Louise Harnby
Marketing manager: Catherine Slinn
Cover design: Shaun Mercier
Typeset by: C&M Digitals (P) Ltd, Chennai, India
Printed in Great Britain by Ashford Colour Press
Ltd., Gosport, Hants

Library of Congress Control Number: 2014935726

British Library Cataloguing in Publication data

A catalogue record for this book is available from
the British Library

ISBN 978-1-4462-9826-8
ISBN 978-1-4462-9827-5 (pbk)

MIX
Paper from
responsible sources
FSC
www.fsc.org   FSC® C011748

At SAGE we take sustainability seriously. Most of our products are printed in the UK using FSC papers and boards.
When we print overseas we ensure sustainable papers are used as measured by the Egmont grading system.
We undertake an annual audit to monitor our sustainability.

To my daughters, with fond memories of their student days.

Contents

Part Five: Producing — 123

Part Six: Polishing — 165

About the author

Dr Lucinda Becker, an award winning Associate Professor in the Department of English Literature at the University of Reading, and University Teaching Fellow, has spent her career committed to the intellectual and professional development of her students. She is a Senior Fellow of the Higher Education Academy and has written numerous successful study skills guides for students. As a professional trainer she also works throughout the United Kingdom and Europe, devising and delivering training in communication and management techniques.

Introduction

For many of us, our final months at university or college are the last time we will be required to write a formal, academic essay. We may use the skills we have learnt, but we will not need to consider that particular format ever again. However, this is not the case for dissertations or reports. Reports will form the mainstay of professional communication for very many graduates, whilst the ability to produce a lengthy written output in response to a business challenge or research activity will be highly prized in both the commercial and academic world.

This is the backdrop against which this book has been written. My aim, as both a university lecturer and a professional trainer, is to produce a guide which is of immediate help to you (whether you are a student or a professional) and also of long-term value as the demands of, first, your academic life and then your professional life become more complex. This guide is about getting good grades, of course, but it is also about making a comfortable and successful transition from studying to the workplace. I am often faced with a room full of newly qualified graduates who have successfully entered upon a career and yet who are devastated to learn that their writing, which was perfectly acceptable when they were students, is not up to the mark now that they are working professionally.

The advice I am offering you is based on my system of 'six Ps': pondering, preparing, planning, pausing, producing and polishing; each of these represents a stage in the process of producing a persuasive piece of writing. You will not spend the same amount of time working through each stage and, depending on your goal and your level of experience, you might find yourself moving through one section quite quickly, whilst in another section you could linger for a significant amount of time. This is all to the good: as your skills develop and your experience grows you will be able to return to just a few key sections of the book as you face each new challenge.

By reading this book you are clearly concerned to save yourself time by getting it right first time, more of the time, and I want to help you in this. That is why the advice I am offering is immediate, relevant and uncompromisingly practical. If you do not need to know a technical term of grammar, I will not bother you with it; if you can achieve impact in several ways, I will offer them all to you so that you can see what suits you best; if there is a quicker, smarter way to do something, you can be sure that I will share it with you. I see us as in this together as we work step by step through the processes which will allow you to achieve your goal: the best possible report or dissertation, based on a sound understanding of how to write with impact.

PART ONE

Pondering

You might reasonably expect a book about writing reports and dissertations to begin and end with writing, but there is much to do before you begin the writing process. It is only by being clear about the task ahead of you and sure about what you aim to achieve that you can move on to produce the best possible report or dissertation.

1

Why a dissertation?

Looking up a quick definition of 'dissertation' in the Oxford English Dictionary, I am told that a dissertation is either a 'discussion, debate' or, with some more recent examples of usage offered, 'a spoken or written discourse upon or treatment of a subject, in which it is discussed at length; a treatise, sermon, or the like'. So, we have some options here: it is clearly a term which can be used to put forward an argument, to support a case being made by its creator or to examine a topic from several angles at some length. The only word that many students would see in an initial glance at the previous part is the word 'length': that is the most important challenge they believe they face. How on earth are they supposed to write so many words, they often ask of me, in varying levels of despair. In reality, the length is only very rarely the problem they expected it to be: by the end of the process they are usually bemoaning the fact that the word count is too low. (I know this might seem unbelievable from where you are now, but it does happen very frequently, I promise.)

Having considered very briefly what a dissertation is, we need to think about why anyone would tackle what can, at first, seem like a daunting task. For many students, they have no choice: dissertations are becoming a far more common compulsory feature of courses in higher and further education. This is, in part, why so much mythology swirls around dissertations. You might have to do one, and it will be in your final year of study, and you do not want to think about it yet, and people have told you that it is the most difficult thing they have ever done, and you will have to write more words than you have written before. ... The list of negatives goes on and on, but when you approach it as we will be doing in this guide, you will see that none of this matters. It is simply another task to be undertaken as part of your academic development and, by its completion, you will surprise yourself by realising that you have produced a body of work which is unique to you and of which you can be inordinately proud.

Top Tip

If the descriptions given in this guide match what you are doing, do not be put off if the term 'dissertation' is not used in your institution. Sometimes what is essentially a dissertation is given another name such as a 'long essay' or 'summative year essay' or some such.

Dissertations are not always compulsory: many students choose to undertake a dissertation because they enjoy the chance to consider a topic in depth, to carry out some research which is more extensive than that required for an essay and to develop their writing skills in a new way. Especially for those undergraduates who hope to move on to a higher degree, a dissertation is their chance to begin to develop those necessary skills. For those who are already undertaking a higher degree (such as a Master's), a dissertation will be a required output; for those who have moved on to doctoral research, the dissertation will seem tiny compared to the mountain of a thesis which they are climbing.

In the commercial world, a lengthy piece of work might be very similar in principle to a dissertation, even though it would not be called by this name. A quick glance at Wikipedia© offers me this definition of a dissertation: 'Dissertations normally report on a research project or study, or an extended analysis of a topic. The structure of the thesis or dissertation explains the purpose, the previous research literature which impinges on the topic of the study, the methods used and the findings of the project.' This rather broader definition seems to me to relate as much to commercial activities as to academic pursuits. It is for this reason that, whilst the report writing sections of this guide will be of most obvious relevance in the commercial world, the guidance offered for dissertations would also be worth perusing by the professional reader. A huge bid document, for example, or an extended business case, may have far more in common with a dissertation than a report.

Top Tip

The advice offered in this guide will be relevant to both academic and commercial writers. As a professional, a lengthy and well-structured write-up of an investigation would not be called a dissertation, but the same principles apply and so the advice offered here is equally relevant to students and professionals. I might refer to one or the other group of writers, depending upon the context, but try to resist the temptation to skip over a section on the assumption that it is not 'for you'.

2

What is distinctive about a dissertation?

Dispelling some fixed but erroneous ideas about dissertations might come in handy here:

It is hugely long: Yes, it is a lengthy piece of written work, but this does not mean that every dissertation is of the same length. Depending on its purpose it might be 8,000 words in length (which might be typical for a dissertation which reflects upon a student's placement learning experience), or 10,000–12,000 words (which could be fairly standard for an undergraduate dissertation in the final year of study) or up to 20,000 – 30,000 words, which would work well as a postgraduate dissertation.

What is important is not so much the length – the word count will have been set to be sufficient for what is required of you – as the fact that, in academia at least, there is a fairly rigid word count. Even if the lengthy piece of work you are producing commercially does not have a word count as such, we do tend to judge by length to some extent, so check if your boss/team/client is used to receiving written output of a certain length. There is no benefit to surprising people by an unexpected word count if there is no reason for it. If you are aiming to produce an academic dissertation, know your word count but also, just as importantly, find out if there is any leeway at all. A 10 per cent leeway might make little difference to a short essay, but it would be about 1,000 words for the average dissertation.

You will also need to assure yourself about what is included in the word count. Is it just the main body of the dissertation, or does it also include the table of contents, the abstract, summary or synopsis, your references section and so forth? You might also note here that word counts have changed slightly in recent years. Whereas there was once no word count, we then moved to a maximum word count and, more recently, it has become far more usual to have a minimum word count as well. The very fact that you are reading this guide suggests that you have the dedication to produce far more than the minimum number of words, but it is still a good idea to know what it is.

It looks like an essay: Yes and no is the rather confusing answer to this one. It is a continuous piece of prose but it is most commonly divided into sections. These sections are usually called chapters, but might be listed as sections instead. Whatever they are named, it does look and feel strange if one reads through a dissertation which has no section or chapter breaks, so make sure that you introduce these into your earliest stages of planning and preparing. Whenever I mark a dissertation which has no section or chapter breaks I always find myself wondering whether the student did not read the guidance notes, or whether he or she lacked confidence in the work to such an extent that chapter headings seemed too bold for what was being said, or whether, perhaps, there is a deeply artistic reason for the break with tradition of which I am unaware. You would not want your examiner to be distracted by any of these stray thoughts, so sticking to the structure you have been asked to produce works best.

Whilst most of the time you will be writing in the same style you would use in an essay, you will be conscious that you want the dissertation to stand as a whole and so you will make sure that it is edited and polished so that it does read through as one persuasive piece of work. Text will, of course, form the basis of a dissertation, but it differs from the traditional essay in that you may be more inclined to include textual options which would feel unfamiliar in an essay. Headings and subheadings, bullet-pointed lists, illustrations, graphs and charts: all of these might be useful additions to your dissertation and in this it can be more like a report than a standard essay.

It has to be divided into chapters: It will certainly be divided, but the divisions might be called sections or parts rather than chapters. Whatever you choose to call the divisions in your dissertation, whether they are parts, chapters or sections, or a combination of these, you need to demonstrate a logical development of both your argument and your material. This will rely on meticulous planning, and I will be helping you with that, but also on your ability to see it as a whole piece of work in and of itself, with a strong, logical thread running right through its centre. You might write as you prepare, making notes on the material you are studying and maybe suggesting where in your dissertation that material might fit, but you would probably avoid writing the actual dissertation until you know where you are going; that is, until it has been thought through thoroughly and planned sufficiently.

A dissertation is based only on original research: The answer to this is simple: no, it is not. Of course you will be carrying out your own investigations and drawing conclusions from the material on which you are working, so in this way it will be unique. A doctoral thesis might aim more firmly towards the goal of making an utterly ground-breaking contribution to the sum of human knowledge, but we are all standing on the shoulders of those who went before: much of your output will be reviewing the existing situation in your topic area, considering the research that has already been carried out, using this to guide your own activities and then coming to some conclusions about what you have witnessed or discovered.

For some dissertation writers, the notion that they have to be original at all points in their work can be a huge hindrance, freezing up their thinking and undermining their ability to produce anything much at all. It is important at this stage that you relax about this. You will find new things to say and you will be contributing to the sum of human knowledge (even synthesising two previously dislocated observations from other pieces of research will do this), but you can feel confident that this will happen.

A dissertation must provide answers: It is only natural that you will want to offer your readers some answers and, of course, it is satisfying for a reader to be led through some interesting areas in which answers are offered, but this issue is the one which most fundamentally divides a dissertation from an essay or a report. In an essay, students are expected to answer questions, even if in some cases they have crafted the question themselves, whereas the main interest in a dissertation will lie not only in the answers, but in the research questions. It would be desirable to plan around research questions as soon as you find some, and it would not be expected that you will answer every question: you may well leave the reader with the exciting feeling that there is more to learn about your chosen topic.

Remember too that a dissertation may form the basis of a discussion at a viva voce examination (a 'viva') and so you will need to be able to defend your points not just in writing, in the dissertation, but also in discussion with experts. This should not deter you from including some discussion points (or research questions) for which you do not provide a firm or fully developed answer, as long as you are ready at your viva to explain to the examiners why you did not pursue that particular line of inquiry beyond the elementary stages of questioning or hypothesising.

Having cleared up some typical fallacies, there is one golden rule about dissertations which I want to share with you before we move on. A dissertation should always be something in which you can take pride. You will probably be dedicating long months of your life to it and it will stay with you as a permanent record of your achievement. I always feel sorry for those students who hand in a dissertation poorly printed out with just a staple holding it together, clearly having run out of time even to proofread it through. All of that work and the end result is something they will probably want to forget. So, let's agree on this now: a dissertation is elegantly written, suitably bound, of the right length and handed in on time. It is an object in which you can take pride for years to come.

3

What are research questions?

The idea of research questions is quite alien to many undergraduates and can be worrisome even for those working at postgraduate level, yet they are important to the success of many activities, including dissertations. In this respect, a dissertation is akin to postgraduate activities, which might be one reason why, if you have a choice, you might opt for a dissertation at under-graduate level: it is good preparation for work you might come to do as a postgraduate.

So, what is a research question? It is the question you ask yourself at some point in your research activity, the question which prompts you to offer your reader an answer and, in many cases, the question which leads on to further areas of study. I have specified here that a research question may come to you 'at some point' because it is not always the first thing which enters your mind: sometimes you find answers and have to work back in order to identify the research question you are in the process of answering.

You will have at least one research question as you embark on a dissertation. This will be the question that led you to consider an area of study and research, even though you might – just from habit – have tried to frame it as a title. Here are some examples of how dissertation titles could be 'back-tracked' to a research question:

- The title 'The timing of crop planting on an arable farm in Devon' would be based on the research question 'How can farmers maximise their crop yield on arable farms in Devon?'
- The title 'The impact of time in Shakespeare's sonnets' would be based on the research question 'Why does Shakespeare refer, both explicitly and implicitly, to the passing of time so often in his famous sonnet sequence?'
- 'The effect of gender on public exam results in Europe' would be based on the research question 'Why do girls seem to be achieving better than boys in education nowadays?'

- The title 'Consider the impact of steel expansion and resonance in the stability of suspension bridge girders' would be based on the research question 'Why do some newly designed bridges tend to sway when too many people walk over them?'

You will probably have noticed straight away that the research questions might, in these cases, have come before the titles or the titles might have come to mind in the first place, and then been unpicked to produce the research question. You might also notice that the research questions are a little vague and unformed; they are more the type of question you might ponder with a friend in casual conversation, rather than being a formal statement of intent.

In each of these examples I have suggested just one research question, but if you were to tease out the implications of the titles further, you would see that several research questions might actually be applicable to each. Taking just the first of these examples, we can see how it might expand to include several research questions at its source:

'The timing of crop planting on an arable farm in Devon' could rely upon several research questions, in addition to the one I have already given, such as:

- Does the climate in Devon affect the timing of sowing and harvesting?

- Which types of crop might be planted so as to produce two harvest periods per year?

- What if the farm were mixed rather than purely arable?

- What would happen to the profit margins if crop timing were to be altered?

- Would crop rotation affect this?

- What impact on labour would arise from altering current practices?

- What are the risks and benefits of arable farming in a new way in Devon?

Already you can see that a plan is almost beginning to emerge, and that is the most important function of research questions in relation to a dissertation: they allow you to control your writing effectively. Although the idea of your topic growing as you find more and more research questions can be scary, one of the techniques you will master is the ability to take control of the process by deciding when you have discovered enough research questions for your purpose. If, as you begin to produce your dissertation, you come to realise that you are going to have too much material (either for your word count or for the central argument you are trying to make), it is far easier to lop off a research question from your plan than it is to try desperately to condense material which you have already spent time producing. We will return to this in the part on planning.

On considering this list of research questions you might suspect, rightly, that there are just too many broad research questions here. If you were writing a book on this topic you might be able to include some answers to all of them, but for a dissertation you are more likely to have to make some judgements as you begin to use these questions to plan. Climate and the type of crop will clearly be important research questions, but you might decide that thinking about the ramifications of crop timing on a mixed farm is outside your remit; similarly, the impact on labour on the farm might seem to you to be too large a topic to tackle within your word count. Both of these, however, would be interesting areas to raise in brief during your dissertation to show that you have considered some tangential areas beyond those which you have been able to cover.

Despite the fact that some of these research questions might have to be abandoned because of the size allowed for your dissertation, the principle of using research questions to drive your progress remains the same. Rather than striving to close down the intellectual pursuit by simply answering a preordained question, as you might do in a brief essay, in a dissertation you are pursuing the research questions where they lead you and only after some consideration and time would you decide which ones to answer fully, which to mention only in passing and which to leave as questions. Some of the most impressive dissertations I have marked have been those where the writer has been confident enough, and intellectually curious enough, to finish the dissertation with a series of research questions which have been raised by the dissertation research and have yet to be answered.

There is a threefold advantage to being able to identify enough research questions that you have a few left unanswered at the conclusion of your work. First, they intrigue the reader, secondly, they might intrigue you enough to inspire you to carry out further research at a higher level, and, finally, money tends to follow research questions. If you can produce a funding application (for postgraduate research, for example) with some really fascinating research questions, you are more likely to be successful.

4

What makes a good dissertation?

If the answer to this question were simple, there would be no need for this guide. Producing an effective dissertation is a challenge and as we work through the process together you will come to learn about what will make your dissertation the best it can possibly be, so for now I will offer you just a few key features which I have learnt make for a good dissertation:

Uniform: It is easy to forget, when you are in the throes of writing, that you are producing one complete piece of work, even if you are tackling its production in several stages. Most of us have lived through the experience of forgetting to put page numbers into a document, or overlooking the labelling of one image or graph, or failing to notice that the font size on our headings or subheadings has changed halfway through. In themselves none of these may matter too much, but they force the reader to assume that you did not care enough to check the dissertation through, which is obviously not the impression you would want to give.

Clear: Your reader will not necessarily be prepared to work very hard to understand you and will not be inclined to care much about what you have to say if you did not seem to care much about it. Never make sweeping generalisations if you can find and then offer your readers full and accurate information; do not rely on assumptions if you can prove your point succinctly and persuasively; try to avoid writing in a way which makes your dissertation hard work to read.

Accurate: There is no getting away from the fact that your dissertation needs to be as near perfect as you can get it with reference to the mechanics of the work. Your language needs to be precise (later chapters in this guide will help with this); your punctuation needs to serve the proper function (again, I can help you with that); your bibliography and references need to be flawless.

So far this list has covered some practical aspects of your dissertation. These might seem to you to be the least interesting features on which to focus, but if you can get into the right frame of mind they can become satisfying. There is something quite soothing about spending an entire afternoon checking that your referencing is accurate; similarly, it can be unexpectedly pleasant to work through your dissertation with a red pen in hand, finding trifling mistakes. Compared to the brainwork of writing, this is relatively easy and you know that every amendment you make will be an easy win: it will improve your work without any great effort on your part except the discipline required to sit down and do it.

The list was also rather severe in tone and approach. Why? Because I do not want 10 per cent of your reader's brain distracted either by having to work too hard to access the fruits of your brain, or by wondering vaguely why you have changed font size, or not labelled something, or why you did not take the time to produce something praiseworthy. I want you to avoid that distraction in your readers because I want their full focus to be on the other, more creative features of a good dissertation, which will be:

Interesting: Your dissertation will be read by someone who can be presumed to have a common interest with you in the area you are exploring, and so it should be easy to keep the attention of whoever is reading and/or assessing it; yet too often dissertation writers forget that, if you cannot engage the interest of the readers, you will find it far more difficult to get your points across. Much of the advice offered in this book is aimed at helping you to capture and then sustain the interest of your readers.

Intriguing: At each stage you will need to challenge yourself to move outside your own sphere of thinking and to consider the experience of the reader: are you raising clear and intriguing research questions? Are you answering them persuasively enough? Will your readers want to take a break from time to time, just to consider all of the interesting points you are making? Right down to the final check of your dissertation, I will be encouraging you to take your readers into account.

Persuasive: You might have noticed that in this list 'readers' are referred to in the plural; this is because you will usually have at least two readers who are assessing your work, and sometimes more, and for a commercial document you could expect to have many more readers. This means that you are being asked to persuade readers with slightly different viewpoints and levels of understanding/interest. You will be able to do this effectively once you have mastered the techniques contained in this guide, but the primary point to accept here is that you are always trying to persuade your readers of something. Even if you are not actively engaged in forming an argument at a point in your dissertation, you are still seeking to persuade them that you can create an impressive dissertation.

Confident: It will not surprise you to learn that there is no instant formula which will give you the type of confidence in your material that you need if you are to come across as intellectually engaging and reliable in terms of the material you offer and the conclusions you draw from your research. Although this confidence takes time to achieve, you have that time as you work through with me the process of producing a dissertation. All you need do now is be aware of it and, if ever you find yourself losing confidence in what you are writing, go back to your plan for a moment and remind yourself of where you have been and the impressive amount of work you have already done.

Although by considering these ideas you are preparing the way for the challenge ahead, it is far later in the process when you might find them most useful. Once your dissertation is written, as you prepare to work through it to edit, polish and proof it, have this checklist to hand so that you can ask yourself if you have met each of these key challenges.

5

When and why would I write a report?

The ability to write a successful report has always been commercially and professionally important: it is now also important for students. Whilst a dissertation might be the only lengthy, fully structured piece of writing you would expect to do at college or university, you are ever more likely to come across report writing as a requirement. The problem with this, for many writers, is that it can catch you out. I regularly teach professionals who are coming to report writing for the first time, sometimes well into a successful career, and they feel as if they are playing catch up, trying to grasp the principles of report writing as quickly as possible so that nobody realises that this is new to them.

What I have noticed across the years is that this response, this sense that somehow you 'should know' how to produce a successful report, is common to all groups I teach, from first-year undergraduates, through to postgraduate researchers, right up to managers in mid-career who feel that somehow they have fallen through the net and that they need to master the art of report writing as rapidly as possible. So that is exactly what I aim to achieve with you in this book. Whether you are a first-year undergraduate or an experienced professional, this guide will help you to master report writing as directly and effectively as possible.

Although the easy answer to the question posed in this chapter's title is 'Someone told me to do it', and this is often the case, it is useful here to go through not just why you might *have* to produce a report, but why you might *opt* to write one. As with dissertations, we can do this by dispelling some myths:

Reports are unlikely to be required of most writers: Reports have become ever more popular over the last decade or so, in both academia and the professional world. Colleges and universities have seen that they can be used to produce crisp, succinct accounts of assessed work, whilst the commercial world has become increasingly used to expecting a report in a diverse range of situations.

Reports are written by scientists and engineers: In times gone past reports were almost the exclusive preserve of scientists and engineers; indeed, 'technical' or 'scientific' were words that would most usually precede the word 'report'. Nowadays the use of reports has widened hugely. They are used to give information, to create a persuasive argument, to showcase projects and to report on commercial activity. The greater your skills in report writing, the easier it will be for you to branch out into other forms of commercial writing, now or in the future. Specifications, business cases, press releases, bids and tenders: all of these rely on the work you are doing here.

Reports are for highly academic writing: It perhaps goes without saying that, when reports were principally scientific or technical, they were also rigid, precise and highly academic in nature. Although you will want to bring intellectual rigour to whatever you are doing, your report might not be the culmination of an academic project. You might be asked to write a short report in order to propose a group project in a class, or you could find yourself writing a more lengthy report on a career placement you have undertaken; these will not be 'traditional' academic reports, but they could be vital to your experience as a student. In the commercial world, any situation might require a report, which could be anything from three to four hundred pages long, or more, but luckily the skills you learn writing one report will be directly transferable to another.

All reports are the same in terms of layout and tone: There are standard layouts for reports, and in specific companies or university departments there may be a standard layout for reports. However, the layout is usually open to some manipulation. For example, whether you include 'conclusions' and 'recommendations' sections separately will depend on what you are trying to achieve, and in some cases they will not appear at all in reports. The tone can always vary, from the strictly impersonal and precise to the engaging and energetic. The trick is to discover what you *have* to do in the report you are required to write, and then decide, from what is still variable, what would suit your purposes best.

Reports are difficult to write: Reports are actually easier to write, in many cases, than essays or dissertations, as long as you are prepared to tackle them head on and not allow yourself to be intimidated by a layout with which you might be unfamiliar or a set of standard requirements which will seem strange at first. The key to success in report writing lies with the planning: plan thoroughly and you will be in the best position to write well. For many of my students, they much prefer report writing to producing essays, once they have got over the initial surprise at the idea of having to write one. For me, once I could write an effective report, I enjoyed the fact that I could use a report style of writing in other documents whenever I wanted, so it expanded my armoury for persuasion in other areas.

A report would not allow me to create an argument: Quite the reverse. A report is perfectly designed to produce a persuasive argument. Unlike an essay, where you hope to bring the readers with you through an argument, in a report you have the option of using headings to guide your readers before they have read a word of the report itself. You can use the same material in a variety of different ways without being criticised for repetition and you can use a plethora of textual options to boost up your effective use of language. A report is the ideal tool for persuasion, once you have mastered the format.

The structure you use should not matter; your work is still important: There is occasionally a slight dismay to be found amongst those who feel that content is all, that their argument and the quality of their material should shine through, regardless of the format in which it is presented. Given that you are investing your time in reading this guide, it is unlikely that you are very strongly of this persuasion, but it is worth considering the reality of the situation. Your principal method of persuasion, the main means you will use to impress your reader, will always be your words, but it would be futile to ignore the fact that headings, bullet points, pictures, graphs, repetition and neatly packaged material also help with this task: a report offers you all of these options.

Reports are rigid in structure and so tend to restrict the writer: You will have gathered by now that this is not a position I would support, but I do recall the first instance in which I had to write a report. Beyond a fairly sketchy plan I had never done more than allow my words to flow as I meandered through an academic argument. I resented the idea that I was being asked to restrict myself to a report format and, if I recall rightly, I was a little intimidated by this new format for my writing. I should confess here that the first report I wrote was not especially good, despite my spending time on it, but then I learned that my writing would only work in a report format if I knew fairly accurately what I wanted to write, and how I was going to organise my material, before I started to write. After that, things got better, but it took time to get to the position where I really enjoyed the power of persuasion that reports offer; I am hoping that this guide will save you some of that time.

Reports are completely objective: This is untrue, and is the most common fallacy about reports. It is true that, in the main body of a report, you would lay down, in as impartial a way as possible, all of the evidence that you have gathered and which is relevant to your argument. Already you can probably spot the subjectivity inherent in a report: *you* are the one who decides which material is to be included, which is less relevant and can go into an appendix, and which can be left out altogether. You decide on the order of material and how much space is given over to it. You seek, through your ordering and writing style, to persuade a reader of something. I would not for a moment advocate that you use reports to deceive or dupe your readers, and it is true that they are designed to provide evidence through which the reader can discern the conclusions, just as you have, but they are still documents produced by highly subjective human beings trying to have their say, so they will never be entirely objective, however impartial you manage to be.

Having established that reports are relevant to the lives of students and professionals, and that mastering report writing will be of benefit to you now and in years to come, it occurs to me that I have not yet described or defined a report. Although most people would recognise one if they saw it, it could be useful to pause here to consider what makes a report.

6

What is distinctive about a report?

This chapter will be shorter than its dissertation counterpart, partly because reports are so widely used that they have taken on a life of their own, with multiple variations in how they are produced and presented. However, there are some standard aspects to reports:

- **Bound**: Although you might not be required to pay out for a commercial binding service, it would be unusual for a report simply to be stapled together; more usually, it would be in a report wallet or bound in some way. Commercial organisations and educational establishments will often have an on-site binding service for this type of document.
- **Visually impressive**: A company logo, the use of colour or an eye-catching font might be used on the front page so as to make a report stand out from the other documents on a reader's desk. Making a front page impressive can be daunting at first, but it will become an enjoyable part of producing your report.
- **Professional looking**: Once you know that you are aiming for a striking front page you then need to avoid the temptation to include so many features that it comes to look amateur or even childish. Inserting a few generalised images and using a really large font is not going to do anything to inspire confidence.
- **Table of contents**: It is not common for a report to have an index and so the table of contents is the way in which your readers will navigate their way around your document. It is therefore vital that you include every heading in the table of contents, even if you have used several levels of heading in the report.
- **List of writers**: For both academic and commercial reports you would expect to include, usually on the front or back of the title page, or on the back cover, if you have one, a list of the writer or writers of the report. This does not sound problematic, but it can be. Most usually, a group of up to three authors will be individually named; for reports with more than three authors the convention would commonly be to name the lead author with the words 'et al.' (short for 'and others' in Latin) after it. This is fine as long as you do not find

that you have written most of the report and yet are listed, on the report and in the archives, as 'et al.'. If you are the lead author, try to ensure that you are listed as such.

- **Contact details**: Even if a report is written by a group of people, or by a department of an organisation or, indeed, on behalf of an entire organisation, it still needs to display some means by which those responsible for the report can be contacted. This might be a postal or email address or a phone number (always making sure that you offer your full phone number rather than just an internal extension number).
- **Distribution list**: For an academic report there may be no requirement to include a distribution list of readers for whom the report is intended. In a commercial organisation the distribution list might be far stricter, with each listed recipient being required to sign off to show that he or she has read the report. In most cases a distribution list will not limit the circulation of a report, which might end up being archived and seen by a multitude of readers over the years, but it is a useful thing to include.

Top Tip

You can only be expected to write for your listed readers, regardless of who else gets hold of your report; it is with this in mind that some report writers include an 'intended reader' outline in their report, listing the qualifications and experience of the ideal reader, so that anyone reading the report will know the level at which it is aimed.

- **Summaries**: Later on in this guide I will be sharing with you the various ways in which a report might be summarised, and the advantages of this to the writer; for now, it is sufficient just to note that some form of summary would usually be expected in a report.
- **Headings and subheadings**: The fact that reports have numbered headings is one of their most distinctive features. There was a time when one could confidently quote the rule that, in a report, each heading had a number and there would be no numbered sections without a heading. Word processing software has changed things so that, in some report templates, you will find that each paragraph is numbered.
- **Masses of white space**: This may seem like a minor point, but actually it can be a defining feature of a good report. Unlike a journal article, where you might be limited to a certain number of pages, or an essay of unbroken text with standard margins, a report gives you the chance to allow your work to 'breathe'. Wide margins, 1.5 spacing or more, plenty of white space around every graph, chart, table and illustration, good-sized section breaks: all of these will automatically make your report more accessible and authoritative.
- **Textual options**: You might use inserts such as illustrations and graphs, but your options do not end here with a report. You are far more likely to see bullet-pointed lists in a report, for example, and you can feel comfortable about inserting text boxes and similar devices. This is one of the pleasures of a report: as long as it helps you to get your message across, you are not limited in the way in which you present your information.

- **Conclusions**: It is common for both technical and general reports to come to a set of conclusions and – in many cases – to also include a set of recommendations. Whereas in an essay this conclusion might be implied by a paragraph beginning with 'In conclusion …' or 'To sum up …' or similar, in a report the conclusions are labelled far more clearly, with a title.
- **Often lead to action**: Not every report will have a recommendations section, but if it does the recommendations could be for the reader ('these are the actions you need to carry out next') or the writers ('this is what we intend to do next'). In an academic report this might be intellectual activity rather than physical actions, such a recommendation that further research is carried out into specific topic areas (these are the research questions that you have had to leave unanswered, perhaps).

7

Should I be asking research questions in a report?

We tend to think of reports as being there to provide answers for the reader, but this does not mean that they are closed-off documents, which do not allow for any speculation at all. Whereas in a dissertation you might find a series of research questions, either implied or explicit, cropping up throughout the work, with some of them answered as the work progresses, in a report there is usually a more formal approach to research questions.

Research questions which you are about to answer might be introduced in the first section of the report, which could be headed in various ways, including 'Introduction' or 'Background'. This is also the section in which I would advise you to include any speculative research questions which you do not intend to answer in the report. So, for example, you might include a sentence such as 'The geographic limitations of the expedition meant that no data could be gathered beyond 3,000 metres above sea level, so the question of oxygenation of algae above that height, whilst interesting, will not form part of this report'. By including a sentence such as this you are giving yourself scope to introduce some research questions which will not be answered in the report, thus showing your extensive interest in the field and also preventing the reader from wasting time wondering about whether or not you are going to pursue an obvious area of activity.

You will also, as I have mentioned, include research questions in the introduction which you do intend to answer in the report. Indeed, in some reports these questions will be clearly laid out in a bullet-pointed list in the introductory section. The purpose of a report is to provide some answers, so unless the writer or writers state anything to contrary in the introduction, the reader can confidently expect that these research questions will be answered by the end of the report.

You might have noticed that in this section I am referring to 'writer or writers of a report'; in doing this I am pointing the way to a problem which often comes up around research questions in multi-authored reports. Whereas in a dissertation, especially an academic dissertation, you would generally expect just one author, in a report, even an academic report, there could be several, and this can lead to problems. Although there are benefits to including a few research questions at the outset that you do not intend to answer fully, if at all, there is little benefit in frustrating your reader by listing a multitude of questions, only a fraction of which will be answered.

I have often seen this happen in multi-authored reports and it tends to be the result either of politeness or good, old-fashioned political bargaining. One writer wants a research question introduced and so is prepared to let another writer introduce a research question. The third writer can feel left out of proceedings and, wanting to make his or her mark on the document, insists that a further research question is introduced. Writer number four has been given additional funding on the basis that a particular area is covered: another research question appears. In practice, this rather ill-formed list of research questions usually has little effect upon the main body of the report; once the writers get started it becomes obvious which questions will lead the research and the resultant output. It does, however, leave the opening section of the report looking unwieldy, so try to keep your research questions down to a reasonable number, or remove some of them if they have clearly become irrelevant by the end of the report.

There are sometimes structural restrictions on dissertations which do not allow for the possibility of appendices or annexes. Reports are not hindered by these restrictions and the addition of appendices or annexes, or both, can help you to manage research questions. You will naturally want to include your key research questions and your principal answers to those questions in the report itself, but you might want to think about including subsidiary research questions, or answers, in the attachments to a report. Thus, for example, you might include your main answers in your conclusions section but then state 'For further options, were the budget to increase, see Appendix A'. In this way you are indicating to the reader that the budget constraints have restricted the solutions that you can offer.

There are also times when you come up with a partial answer. In a dissertation this might be a tantalising point to include in the final sections of the work, whereas in a report you might choose instead to state in your report, 'We made a brief analysis of the material in the Folger Shakespeare Library and then decided to focus on the Bodleian Library resources instead. For details of our preliminary findings from the Folger, please see Appendix B'. This means that your work is not lost but it does not muddy the waters of what you are trying to achieve in the report. It might also give the reader an idea for a new research project based on your preliminary work, so if you intend to pursue it yourself after the publication of the report you might want to reduce potential complications by making mention of it but not including the appendix.

Top Tip

I will be looking with you at the use of report attachments in more detail later in this guide, but it is worth introducing here an old adage for you to think about. Report writers are sometimes counselled that the best outcome is the shortest possible report with the longest possible set of appendices and annexes. Whilst this may not invariably be good advice, it does have some merit as a rule of thumb. Attachments to reports are used to leave the way clear for only the most important material, analysis and conclusions to be included in the report itself. Right from the planning stage you need to have in the back of your mind that you can place any subsidiary material in an appendix or annexe.

PART TWO

Preparing

Now that you are clear about where we are going, it is time to think about the moves to make to get there in the most productive way, maximising the result for your efforts and using the skills and support you already have in place to greatest effect.

8

Devising a strategy

There would be no point in denying that the days after you have been asked to produce a report or dissertation can find you feeling anxious about the task in front of you. In the case of an academic report, you have probably been aware for some time that this would be required of you as part of a project; for a commercial report, you might be given some detail and told to get on with it, or offered an example or template to help you and then left to your own devices. In the case of a dissertation, you might have opted to undertake the challenge or, especially with an academic dissertation, you have known that this would form part of your course of study right from the outset. Whatever your situation, it can be daunting to think of what lies ahead, and you might very naturally procrastinate for some time before you take the plunge and really start to focus on the task.

This can be a good thing, as long as it does not go on for so long that you run out of time to produce the final document. Some procrastination can be useful, relieving your initial stress and giving you time to get your mind around the fact that you are about to undertake this feat. (If that sounds a little dramatic, ask any finalist how an undergraduate dissertation felt, or any graduate recruit how their first report felt.) Assuming that you do not let this stage go on for too long, the only downside to it may be the way in which unfocused procrastination can blow you off course. Although it may not seem like it at the time, you will be mulling over your dissertation or report even as you avoid actually doing anything much about it.

If we accept that we all tend to think about the next challenge, even as we plot to evade it, we come up against a potential problem. If, during this pre-planning stage, you are idly asking all of your friends about their experiences in this area, or asking your academic or professional mentor for some quick advice, or planning out in your head roughly how the timing might work out, you are actually doing the work that you are trying to avoid and doing it badly. You will end up less clear about what you have to do next and far less sure about how to achieve your goal.

So, procrastination can be a good thing, but only if it is structured procrastination, and here is how you go about it:

- Only ask for targeted help.
- Think about how you will time the challenge.
- Return to your topic occasionally.
- Decide on a writing strategy.

By thinking about each of these points in turn you can transform your unproductive procrastination time into an opportunity to ambush yourself and progress with the task.

Targeted help: Asking your friends, your academic mentors or your colleagues to share their experience and offer you general advice on producing a successful report or dissertation is a bit like asking for help with a fear of flying. The advice you are offered is likely to be vague or irrelevant to what you are trying to do; there is also the almost irresistible urge to tell scare stories. Before you can stop it, you will have received a mass of conflicting and unhelpful advice, even though it was sincerely meant, and enough instances of things going dreadfully wrong that you are even more reluctant to get on with the job.

There is an easy way to preclude these possibilities. You could, of course, just resolutely refuse to mention your dissertation or report, but this is extremely difficult to do if you are worried about it. Instead, you might take the more productive option of ensuring that all of the help you get is relevant. Find specific questions to ask and just stick to them. You will find that the advice you receive is useful and you will also be reminded that most people prefer to answer a specific question rather than trying to wrack their brains for general advice.

Questions you might like to ask, for a dissertation, could include:

1. How did you work out your research questions?
2. Did you have to narrow down your topic?
3. Did you find the word count adequate?
4. Did your title change as you went along?

For a report, your questions might also include:

1. Where/how did you get your report bound?
2. Did you find decimal notation confusing?
3. How do you tend to use appendices and annexes?
4. How did you tackle making a summary?

You will no doubt find additional questions, but a list made at the outset can be useful as people begin to offer advice or ask how you are feeling about the project.

Top Tip

If you are in a competitive environment, where many of your peers are also writing a report or dissertation, it can be difficult for everyone to recall exactly where a good idea originated. You might not want to give out all of your best thoughts on topic areas before you have firmed up your dissertation or report title.

Timing strategy: Some people love planning their time, whereas others find it stressful, so you will probably already know whether this particular strategy is likely to work for you. The time given over to dissertations and reports varies, of course, but the same tactic can be used for both. Whether you have three weeks to complete a project and write up a report or a year to work up a dissertation, you could produce a rough timetable showing how it might fit into the rest of your activities.

This approach could have several benefits. The first and most important of these is that it could help you to stay calm. Rather than a vague, queasy feeling about the challenge you are about to face, you will have a reassuring sense of how it can be met within the time you have available. Secondly, you will know when you aim to undertake activities in relation to your dissertation or report. This way, you can build in some 'time off' before you actually get down to doing anything; equally, you can schedule your tasks in such a way that you can take regular breaks every now and then. Pausing in the process can be hugely beneficial, as long as you know when you are to resume the challenge.

Top Tip

If the thought of taking time off from the task is making you feel uneasy, be firm with yourself about the need to take a break. Our brains need time to assimilate and categorise material and our imaginations need time to consider how best we can formulate an argument that is not only sound, but also engaging. You need not see time away as 'time off' – your brain is still mulling over possibilities and will not let you down when you return.

You can share your schedule with your mentors, friends and colleagues whenever you like, so that supporters know when you are likely to be tied up and when you will be free to work on other things. This might sound unrealistic if you are working in a commercial setting, but you could be surprised at how willing colleagues are to leave you alone, as much as they can, if you let them know in advance when you need the time to concentrate (and you are prepared to return the favour). If you are working in a team on a project which will lead to a report or dissertation, and you are the one to suggest a timing strategy, those working with you will respond positively – they may never have thought of taking such a structured approach before – and by leading this move you will have a fair degree of leeway to ensure that the schedule fits your needs well.

The final benefit is long term. By making a schedule you will know not just that you can complete in time, but also what type of activity – preparing, planning, researching, writing, editing, polishing, checking and so forth – needs to be done at each stage. You will also know how long you have allowed for each of these. If you have several months before completion, such as if you are producing an academic dissertation or working on a three-month commercial project, you might begin with a long-term schedule (which might be little more than a timeline of requirements) which is followed by a far more detailed schedule for the last few weeks.

Top Tip

I have seen students and professionals do this very successfully, and sometimes with extremely detailed schedule for the last stages, with every day included on the chart with activity attached or a day off from the task indicated. You will learn what works best for you, but do not be afraid to be as detailed as suits your needs.

Making a schedule is useful to many writers, so even if you tend not to be a keen planner, you may want to have a go just once, in case you find it helpful. Although there is reassurance to be gained from an organised-looking plan which seems to prove that you have enough time to produce a successful report or dissertation, you will need to remain flexible in the way you use it. If things do not go perfectly to plan, try to avoid giving up altogether, but rather rework the schedule so that you can still move effectively towards your completion date. That completion date is not going to move, however difficult it is to reach it, and reworking your plan allows you to see in black and white that, although you have a busy two weeks coming up, you will then be back on course.

Returning to your topic: I am suggesting here that you reexamine your topic area from time to time during this early stage in your preparations, rather than returning to your title. This is because, at this point in the process, it can be counterproductive to have decided upon a final title. Even if you have had to submit a dissertation or report title for the purposes of an academic course, or your line manager has given you a title or approved yours, there will always be some flexibility. So, even if you have a putative title written down somewhere, remember that it is no more than a working title and try to keep an open mind, remembering that you may want to refine the title as your ideas develop.

Top Tip

One way to keep this open-minded approach is to ensure that, when you write down the title at this early point, you write down a series of key words from the title rather than the full title as it has been laid out. All of the information will still be there for you to ponder, but it will not feel set in stone.

Suggesting you return to your topic every now and then is a little disingenuous of me. I know that, whether you mean to or not, that topic will be swirling around in your mind somewhere. This is the time when you suddenly wake up with a great idea about how to begin the first paragraph, or you run to a notepad during a film so as to jot down an idea you want to include or – worst of all – you have an entirely unexpected worry about how a particular section will work, just when you are sitting in a meeting or a lecture and so not in much of a position to do anything about it but worry.

What I am suggesting is not this type of involuntary returning, but rather a more proactive and productive reinterrogation of your topic area from time to time. You might do this every few hours or every few days or even weeks, depending upon your schedule. Each time you do it, take a blank piece of paper and put the key words which occur to you from the title in the middle of the page and then, around this central circle, jot down any ideas which occur to you about these key terms. You are not, in this brainstorm, trying to plan anything; you are just letting your ideas form naturally.

What is often most interesting about this process is what you leave out and what you repeat. A key word which you keep forgetting to jot down might give you pause for thought about how vital/interesting that aspect of your topic will turn out to be; a thought that comes to you again and again (which will be obvious when you look back at several of these sheets in order) must be something that you seriously consider as one of your key areas for inclusion.

Although this will not be a plan, it will be an inspiration and it will be helping your mind, without much effort on your part, to begin on the process of sifting and arranging your data and your overarching argument. The only time it can become counterproductive is when you decide to return to your topic and sit down with a pristine sheet of white paper which resolutely stays pristine and white for ten minutes. This can be most frustrating and a little scary. This is when online brainstorming can help.

I referred earlier in this section to the jotting down of ideas around a few key words: this is a form of brainstorming which you could carry out by yourself or, if you thought it might be useful, with a group of friends or colleagues. If you are sitting alone and no ideas come to mind, you can find yourself rapidly losing confidence in your topic and in your ability to produce the finished report or dissertation.

This is where you could try online brainstorming. Gather together a group in your email address book, with perhaps half a dozen people to start with, all of whom will be supportive of what you are aiming to achieve. Send them an online brainstorm email. The first time you do this you will have to explain the two rules: you can only send an email of a couple of lines, and they can only reply with a few lines. With these rules you achieve two things instantly: you have focused your mind on the real problem that is holding you up (before this you might not have realised where the problem was) and you will ensure that your respondents do not try to write your report or dissertation for you in their reply. So, you will be hoping for replies such as references to journal articles which could give you answers, or a book chapter which would provide evidence for your theory, or for someone to tell you that they tried a particular method or approach years ago and it did not work for them in these circumstances, or perhaps you would be offered the name of a person who is expert in the field and might be willing to help you.

Online brainstorming makes you feel good, both as the sender and the recipient of these emails. I always enjoy receiving them. I make a cup of tea, sit down and open the email, fully ready to respond as best I can to whatever the problem turns out to be. It is flattering to be asked your opinion and it is nice to know that you are not the only person who sometimes struggles to move on to the next stage of a project. I have three separate brainstorm groups in my email address book and I use them for different aspects of my academic and professional life. I love the feeling of being able to send an email and then legitimately be able to abandon a project for the rest of the day; I also feel hugely supported when the emails come back, and they always contain something that will help me to move ahead.

Top Tip

As you can see, online brainstorming is a good way to work up some ideas and share inspiration. It is also a great way to procrastinate whilst still feeling that you are actively working towards your goal. If you have simply run out of ideas and energy at any point, sending around a brief brainstorm email means that you can leave your report or dissertation to one side for a little while and wait for some replies to get you going again.

Decide on a writing strategy: Although I am suggesting that you decide on a strategy, actually for most of us it is more a case of recognising what we already do when we write or, indeed, when we carry out any compulsory task in life. You are likely to be either a 'steady and controlled' writer or a 'fast and frantic' writer. The steady and controlled writer will plan well in advance (as might the fast and frantic writer) and will then work methodically through the process of producing a report or dissertation, regularly producing some written material, perhaps in draft form for rewriting later, and will end up with plenty of time to check and polish the finished result.

The fast and frantic writer may or may not make a plan, but is more likely to put off the task of actually writing, even if he or she is fairly sure about what needs to be said and how it might be expressed. This writer is the sort of person who writes a paper on the train on the way to a conference, or who stays up all night to complete a report. Polishing and checking does not come easily to this type of writer, and may be left until the very last moment, if it is done at all.

Neither of these approaches is necessarily better or worse than the other; there is, however, a problem of perception. Steady and controlled writers are often intensely irritated if they are asked to work alongside fast and frantic writers, but then fast and frantic writers find the steady approach difficult to fathom. There is no denying, also, that there is some pride involved here. Steady and controlled writers will sometimes look down on fast and frantic writers as being less professional, whilst the fast and frantic writers can sometimes be a little attention seeking, masking their fear of the task in a dashing race to the finish line.

You may already know the type of person you are, but two aspects of your writing life might have distorted your view. If you have been in a position where you have had to write at the last minute for your work or your academic course, this will have led you to be fast and frantic even though you might naturally be more of a steady and controlled writer. Secondly, if you have not been encouraged to plan you might have become someone who writes in order to think, but this is not the same thing as being steady and controlled. The steady and controlled writer will plan well in advance and then begin to write early, whereas the person who writes in order to see their thoughts clearly will tend to begin to write early too, but not to any formed plan and not in an especially methodical way.

In my experience, those who write in order to structure their thoughts tend to do so because they have not been encouraged to plan using a planning method which suits both the task in hand and the project which is underway. They can end up wasting their time rewriting and editing their written output, time which could be saved if they were to get all of their thoughts in order by planning before they write. Although you will know what suits you best, I would urge you to try planning before you write, with as detailed a plan as you like, just to see whether this saves you time and offers an improved result. For many writers this will be the case, so it is worth trying.

I will be urging you in this guide to take time to consider your subject area, to spend time planning what you are going to write, to spend yet more time editing and polishing what you have produced. None of these processes will hinder your natural style. If you are a fast and frantic writer you will simply telescope all of the activity until the last possible moment, but you will still be able to do it all in time.

Top Tip

If you know that you are a fast and frantic writer by nature, but this approach actually makes you uncomfortable, leaving you exhausted by nervous tension by the end of writing, you might want to include some 'dummy deadlines' in any writing schedule you make for yourself. Although it might sound strange to put a deadline of your own making into a schedule, one which is some time ahead of the actual deadline for completing your report or dissertation, it seems to work surprisingly well for those who would like a slightly less nerve wracking life.

Over the years your writing strategy will change; this is inevitable as you discover new techniques and develop your own working practices. You will find that the strategies I have explored with you here might work well for you under some circumstances and less well under others. You might adopt a strategy now which, with more experience, you refine to suit your needs more fully. Whatever you end up doing with them, the strategies I have mentioned in this chapter can be applied, as can much else in this book, to any type of writing and, indeed, to most types of project you are likely to undertake in the coming months and years.

9

Gathering material

The ability to focus is going to be essential to your efficiency in the task ahead of you, but pressure of time should not be allowed to exclude the pleasure to be taken in that task. I recall the first year of my doctorate, when I was just beginning to feel comfortable with working in the archives. I had to drive some distance to study in the Bodleian Library and I had to do this during school hours so that I could pick my children up, and I was working as a freelance trainer so my days in the library were hard fought for and precious. Each time I was there I saw a fellow doctoral researcher working away, as she did every day of the week, and as I left I would see her sitting on the library steps, in the sunshine, eating her sandwiches. I so envied her – the time, the leisure to explore the archives, the space to think.

I still envy her that experience, but my envy is now tempered with the realisation that I was, of necessity, utterly focused on what I had to achieve in each visit, and ruthless about not wasting a minute of that precious time. I think the experience probably made me a more efficient researcher; it certainly made me a speedier writer. If I was to be completely honest, I suspect that my envy was also slightly mollified by the fact that she left academia as soon as she had gained her doctorate: she confided in me that she was sick to death of the archives. She has since gone on to an interesting career elsewhere, so we both got our happy ending.

My point is that you will be able to take pleasure in a certain amount of rootling around in your material before you form it into an argument for a report or dissertation, but this will be far more satisfying if you know that you have a firm plan to which you are working. The first stage of this plan is about how you handle what you are reading (or plan to read) or the experimental work you are conducting.

Categorise your reading and experimental matter

All of us who have produced a report or a dissertation know the pressure of a mass of reading material which must be conquered but which resists our best efforts. This might include other reports or dissertations, articles in journals or on the internet, books and book chapters and so forth. For scientists, this will also include not only examining experimental findings already achieved by others, but also devising their own laboratory activities in the most efficient way, especially with the scarcity of available laboratory time which can be the bane of scientists' lives. For social scientists there could be a mass of data, both quantitative and qualitative, which needs to be sourced, judged and either discarded or, perhaps, expanded by further research activity.

With so much to consider, it is vital that you take control of your reading material, even before you have made detailed notes on it. We all live with piles of books and articles to hand and a plethora of additional material which we could access easily through a library or resource centre, or instantly through the internet. This written material needs to be tamed, and you can do this by recognising categories into which you can slot every single piece of material you encounter:

Essential

How to spot this material: These are sources which you will want to keep for most of the time that you are working on your report or dissertation. They may be books which you have bought, or printed out pages from the internet, or small style guides from your organisation.

How to use it: Try not to be a snob about this material: if you find it useful and it is sound as to the information it is giving, then use it even if it is not the most impressive text you own. I kept a popular history book beside me throughout my doctoral research. It was frowned upon in academic circles but it was readable, reliable and inspirational. If you have something similar, keep it close.

Pull apart

How to spot this material: This is in some ways the most satisfying material with which you will work. It might be just a couple of pages from an internet site, or a collection of essays, only one of which is relevant, or a book which you know has just one or two chapters which are vital to you. For experimental data this might be the one element of experimental results which is useful whilst the rest must be discarded. It is pleasurable because you can work through it quickly, gathering useful information which will help to form your ideas as you go.

How to use it: There are two rules with this type of material. Do not allow yourself to be led astray into making notes on a larger proportion of the material than you had originally planned, unless you have very good reason: if you planned to consider the two most relevant chapters, then try *only* to make notes on those chapters.

Secondly, do not let your material lie fallow for too long. If you are working in a library or resource centre, the chances are that you will make photocopies of the pages you need and leave the source material where it is; on the internet, you might print off just a couple of pages. Resist the temptation to put these shiny new copies into a plastic wallet only to ignore them; force yourself to make notes on them or use a highlighter pen to work through them for relevance before they are filed away. Ideally, your notes on them would include details of how you see this material fitting into your report or dissertation. You might change your mind, but a series of 32 plastic wallets with no indication of how the material might be used will be extremely off-putting later, so try to get into good habits early on.

Mining

How to spot this material: Material for mining can be very useful but it can also be tricky to handle. These are the sources where you are just going to glance through the index or table of contents, or use search engine keywords to see if your topic is mentioned anywhere, so that you can dive straight in, grab a good quote and leave, ready to include this material and reference it in your bibliography or references section.

How to use it: Gathering snippets of material for brief references in this way is not cheating. If you are making a convincing argument, then you are bound to find others who agree with you. You do not need to read an entire book or website in order to prove this; the odd quotation will suffice, as long as you read enough to contextualise the quote and assure yourself that the writer is actually in agreement with your viewpoint. Your bibliography indicates the breadth of your reading; it does not require that you have read each piece of source material in its entirety. It is better to boast of all of the sources you have examined than to omit a source because you have only quoted from it briefly and then find yourself having plagiarised through false modesty.

Irrelevant

How to spot this material: This category can cause some anxiety. It is not always easy, especially if you are new to a topic area, to be confident enough to discard material which is not useful for your purposes. It is made even more difficult to do if an esteemed colleague or reliable mentor seems to have recommended the material. However, you must be bold here. These books lurk around the place making you feel bad about yourself and what you are trying to do, so you must get them out of your sight.

How to use it: Remember that it is possible that your colleague or mentor gave you the wrong reference. I recall buying a book by a respected scholar in my field on the recommendation of my supervisor. I spent a year feeling guilty because I could not see its relevance – a year of my life when, if I had been brave enough to ask, I could have saved myself all of the guilt. I had bought the wrong book.

Remember also that some books can be supremely helpful to some writers and yet leave you cold because you do not get along with the style in which it is written, or it does not quite meet your research needs. It is also worth admitting that some academics and experts, however brilliant they are, just do not write very well and so make their readers work much too hard for every point they are trying to grasp.

So, be firm with this category. If you have double checked and you did write down the correct reference, but you are finding the material unhelpful or impenetrable, despite several efforts to come to grips with it, take it back to the library or make a note of the website address and then put the pages you have printed out to one side, ideally somewhere away from your main reference files. The material is not going to get lost; it will still be in the library, on the internet or in your files if you need it later, but the chances are that you will not need it, and by being decisive you will not have to be distracted by it on a daily basis.

Entertainment

How to spot this material: This category includes anything that you read for pleasure – maybe the novel you read before you go to sleep at night, the magazine to which you regularly subscribe or the websites which you enjoy.

How to use it: Your attitude to this material is likely to change if you are producing a report or dissertation over a lengthy period. As your language becomes more elevated, academically or professionally, and whilst you are reading and digesting regular amounts of specialist material, you might find your normal light reading a little too light. It might be difficult for you to settle to your novel or magazine; you might even find yourself vexed by grammatical errors in the websites you usually enjoy.

Despite this it is important, if you can, for you to persevere and try to find some leisure material that you can still enjoy. (If the worst comes to the worst, I found audiobooks through headphones sent me off to sleep nicely during my dissertation). The reason this is so important is that your brain needs some downtime every day; if you read work or study material last thing at night, or on a train journey when you would normally relax, you will find the process more arduous and your efforts could be less rewarding.

Top Tip

Why not use these categories right away? Put your current stock of books into separate piles which reflect each of these categories. That way you will see in an instant just how useful this approach can be – and next time you are in the library you will probably have some books to put confidently back on the shelf!

Funnel information productively

Controlling your source material into piles according to its use is just the beginning of sifting material so as to become an effective information gatherer. The skills you are developing now will support you in many activities throughout the rest of your life, so they are certainly worth acquiring. Part of learning to funnel effectively is knowing how to use your time to bring you different benefits. There will be times (of the day, of the week, of your entire project) when you are full-steam ahead and ploughing through material with no problems at all; there will also be times when you are tired, perhaps confused, maybe just a touch downhearted about what you are doing.

When you are in the lower energy phase it can be a fruitless task to try to make notes or plan the next stage of your project, but there is something you can do which will always pay dividends: you can work on your reading and research notebooks.

Reading and a research notebook: These notebooks are the secret weapon of many a successful professional (the sort of colleague who can always put a finger on exactly the right resource, who is never short of an idea when asked); they are also used by canny academics who know that nothing need ever be lost when it comes to research.

These notebooks will be hardback and A5 in size and you will probably find that you are carrying them around with you for much of the time if you are actively engaged in a project; they will at least be close to hand on your desk. You will use the reading notebook to jot down every reference to potential source material you come across. These could include websites you hear about, an author or researcher whose work is mentioned in passing, some experimental findings which were discussed at a meeting, an internet site which you keep hearing mentioned. You will also be able to note references from bibliographies in texts on which you make notes, especially your 'pull apart' and 'mining' texts.

Your research notebook will be eclectic in content and will sometimes be therapeutic rather than simply an information gathering exercise. In your research notebook will go all of the ideas about your project that come to you in the shower, or when you are watching television, or sitting in a meeting or seminar. These ideas will be no more than jottings such as 'Check Hall's text on survey methods', 'Add random trial data to Section Two?', 'Check out the journal *History*, Jan 2008 issue' or 'Ask Ana about the Bodleian exhibition – relevant for Chapter Two?'. These are clearly not complete thoughts: they are just a series of 'notes to self' which you can work through in one of your less high energy moments, deciding whether or not to pursue them further or allowing them, in one of your higher energy moments, to inspire you to plan a section, or track down a source, or begin an email exchange with a colleague.

These notebooks will not be static: you will add to them regularly and get into the habit of turning to one or other of them whenever a source is mentioned or an idea comes up. If you draw a margin in the books it allows you to work them effectively. When you come across a reference or idea, you will note it down. Leave a few lines under your note and then rule a line across the page; you can then leave it there as you get on with other things. When you have a 'tidying up session', which will sometimes be when you have run out of inspiration elsewhere, you can return to your notebooks and work on them.

Top Tip

Reading and research notebooks need not necessarily be physical, hardback books; they can just as easily be in virtual form. There are many devices, from your laptop to your tablet to your phone, which will allow you to do what I am suggesting here. Whatever makes you feel most comfortable is the way to go with this.

This work might involve looking up some source details so that you can order a book from your resource centre, or emailing a colleague for a more precise reference, or noting that an idea that you had several weeks ago can now be ignored, or has been used in your project. In your higher energy moments you will take this work further and actually work on an idea for a while, perhaps roughing out a plan of how it might affect your project, or you could take some of the books/journals off the shelves and make notes on them, or check out some internet references.

Once you have done some notebook work you will be able to use the margins. Against each item you have considered or explored, you can make notes in your reading notebook margins such as 'Not needed', 'No good' and 'Done'. You then get a good sense of which sources are irrelevant, which are simply poor sources and which you have made notes on. In your research notebook your marginal indicators might include notes such as 'Won't work', 'Chapter Four', 'Included' or 'See later' (if you have repeated an idea elsewhere). When you have completed each marginal section on a page (of, in this example, your research notebook) it could look something like this:

TABLE 1.1

Yes – planned into report	Nursing Today – was there an article in April on new wound dressing techniques? Could I copy their data mining techniques?
Sorted	Check with Tom about the seminar in May – go together?
No – ignore	Does the Royal College of Nursing endorse home care for ulceration? Include this in Section Three perhaps?
Yes – planned into report	Should I discuss Durham Report? Relevant? New ideas for Section Eight?
No good	August Conference – why did they mention Hennings' technique – what is it?
Internet report copied	Case studies in Kent – worth a trip? Or check internet report?

Once you have reached the stage when each marginal section is complete on both sides of a page, it is useful to snip off a right hand corner of the page so that you know that each thought and idea on that page has been addressed and the necessary action taken. That way you will not lose sight of where you are in the research process.

 **Top Tip**

Although this might seem like a minor act – just getting a couple of books in which you note down references and ideas – your reading and research notebooks can become much more than that; if they work for you, let them become a mainstay of your project. I recall walking in procession to gain my doctorate, with people congratulating me on the achievement – I had completed a thesis and would now be a doctor. This was a momentous moment, yet one of the happiest private thoughts I had as I walked up to graduate was that I had snipped off the corners of every single page in my reading and research notebooks.

Before we move on from the idea of reading and research notebooks it is worth considering briefly the range of benefits they might bring you:

- They reduce stress by offering you guaranteed data capture at all times. Once a reference or idea is noted in the book, you can relax knowing that you will not lose that thought. The relief of never having to wake up worrying that you have lost a good idea from the day before should not be underestimated.
- By putting your sources and project/research ideas in the same place you can organise your notes more efficiently.
- Your notebooks will help you to sift information. The structure of each page forces you to make a decision: are you going to run with this idea or should it be shelved? Is this reference useful to you or would more work on it be a waste of your time? I found that I became far more bold and decisive once I had these notebooks; my confidence as a researcher and a writer grew as a result.
- Nothing is lost once it is in your notebooks, because nothing is actually crossed out, and this brings long-term benefits. You will be able to return to your notebooks in the months and years to come. Whenever you want new inspiration in an area, or at those times when you have a vague recollection of having read or researched something on a topic, your notebooks will be there to help you.

Top Tip

Some people prefer just to have one book in which they either include all references to potential sources and research ideas; some like to start with sources at the front and then turn the book over in order to begin recording research ideas at the back; some would always rather have separate books. You might want to experiment to see what works best for you.

Make notes effectively

You are likely to have plenty of experience in making notes – most of us do. As students we take notes from lectures, jot down ideas from books and journals, and trawl through the internet for useful information. As professionals we might add to this experience taking notes at meetings, condensing papers at conferences and composing emails in response to queries. All of these activities give us some valuable skills, but they can also give us bad habits. This is only logical: a few additional notes taken about a meeting will not matter greatly; a rambling email is not a good thing but it is unlikely to be calamitous; notes to ourselves during conferences can be as loose as we like.

Once you are working on a report or dissertation your purpose changes slightly: your aim is to produce the best possible result from the briefest, most relevant notes. Notes which go nowhere, have no relevance and will end up unused at the end of the process simply represent a waste of your time, time which could have been spent actually writing the document, or editing and polishing it. I am not suggesting for a moment that you rely on inadequate notes, just that you work from the most efficient notes you can produce.

There is a three step guide to getting this right:

Know where you want to go

You need a clear purpose before every information gathering session, whether it is interviewing a subject, carrying out an experiment, reading a book or searching the internet. This is not, as you might expect, something that you discover just before you swing into action. It is a longer process, driven by the notes you have made to yourself in your reading and research notebooks, the work you have carried out previously and the structure that is beginning to emerge for your end product.

Time taken before each information gathering session to straighten out your thoughts and focus on the task ahead is not time wasted. There are several different approaches you might take to this. Some people like to jot down two or three key research questions to which they are hoping to find answers in an information gathering/processing session. Others find this too broad and write down far more specific questions. Some prefer to make a draft plan of a section of their report or dissertation, knowing that it will probably alter later, but finding it helpful to make notes to the backdrop of a plan.

It is often possible to categorise information gathering sessions in terms of their relation to your purpose rather than just in relation to the type of material you are considering. This list gives some of the purposes you might be trying to achieve, although you will probably be able to add more of your own as your ideas develop. You might be making notes so as to:

- Inform your views in general terms about a topic area.
- Get an overview of one aspect of your report or dissertation.
- Focus down on the fundamental material for one or more chapters or sections.
- Gain an insight into a single perplexing aspect of your area.
- Confirm something that you thought you already knew.
- Strengthen or develop your argument in an area.
- Refute an argument which someone has made about your topic area.
- Grab a quote to support a point you are trying to make.

However you do it, ensuring that there is some overview in your mind of what you are aiming to achieve will help you to focus, and will give you the confidence to relax that focus from time to time. If you know where you are going, and, as importantly, why you want to be there, you will get a sense as you go along that you are nearer to your goal than you were, and this will leave you feeling happier about spending a few minutes every now and then just pondering your area and taking a wider view: now that you are immersed, in a structured way, in your material, is there anything out of the ordinary that strikes you? Are there any other avenues that seem to be appearing before you?

Top Tip

If new areas of research do seem to be opening up to you as you carry out an experiment or make notes on your sources, avoid being blown off course by them at that moment. Instead, jot down the idea or possible new direction in your research notebook; that way it is safe and you are free to focus back on the task you have set for yourself.

Know how to get there

Although you will have ensured at the outset that you are clear about where you want to go, it is a good idea, every now and then, to check back to the overview, draft plan or set of tasks you noted down then. This reminds you not only of where you are going, but also of why you want to be there. In this way, you will be ready to make a judgement on how fruitful your work is being. If, for example, you are an hour into a three-hour session when you check and find that you have only covered one-fifth of what you had intended to do, at the very least you can reassess the situation for a few moments and decide whether the material is leading you in a relevant direction, which you should follow even though it is off plan – this happens – or whether you should move on firmly from where you are now in order to gain momentum again with the overall task.

I gave an example there of being an hour into a three-hour session, and it is to timing I would like to turn with you next. Sometimes the time you have in which to gather and process information is dictated by circumstances such as only being able to book a certain amount of lab time, or having a free morning before work meetings or trying to squeeze in a couple of hours' work between lectures. Often, however, you are in a position to decide on your own timing. Even if you are used to working and/or studying hard, it may not be the best approach simply to jump into sessions which last several hours at a time. Instead, as with so much else in life, it is better to take baby steps before you walk and then run.

The first thing you will need to do is to assess your current work rate. Depending on your discipline and the end product, take an activity which you will regularly be undertaking as part of preparing to write your report or dissertation; this might be working through and writing up experimental work, survey or focus group work, transcribing interviews or making notes from written or online sources. As you carry out the activity, note down how much you can achieve in the first fifteen minutes (how many pages of notes, how many words of interview subscribed) and move on, making a note every fifteen minutes of how much is being achieved. For most people there is a sudden drop-off in one of these fifteen minute segments, and this represents the point at which you will begin working much less efficiently.

You might never have realised before that your concentration dips at this point, but now you know you will be ready to improve the length of your productive work rate. Do not try simply to push through the dip; you will be able to do it but it is unlikely that you will achieve your best afterwards. If your schedule allows, take a break at this point and move right away from the activity. This is the perfect time to make a drink, go for a walk, or bask in the sunshine. Make sure that it is a brief break, though – a few minutes should suffice – and ideally do something which gives your eyes as well as your brain a rest.

Go back to the task, refreshed, and check again every fifteen minutes to make sure that you take a break the next time your work rate dips. If you are planning to work for more than three hours, you will need to check every ten minutes after the first three hours as your work rate might dip more quickly. This might seem like a lot of breaks to take, but actually a few minutes away from the task will result in such an improved output that it is worth it, and it becomes a regular habit quickly, so does not feel disruptive.

Top Tip

There is no need to worry if you cannot manage more than thirty minutes, even fifteen minutes, when you first monitor yourself in this way. You will find that, as you continue to carry out these activities, your productive time will increase rapidly. This is especially true if you have not written or made notes extensively for some time. For example, I can happily spend six hours a day writing a book once I am in the flow of it, but a break of a few months would send me straight back to feeling brain mushed after an hour.

The 'Top Tip' above is the result of one of the breaks I am suggesting that you take. Realising that I was approaching the second hour of writing, and knowing that my output would dip dramatically at this point if I did not take a break, I have just had the pleasure of sitting in my garden, drinking a cup of tea in the shade of an apple tree and wondering how it can be 28°C in September. As I sat there, I recalled how demoralised I was when I first came to dissertation writing and started to time myself like this. I seemed to get worn out so quickly, and rubbish flowed effortlessly from my fingertips after a startlingly short amount of time. It was a huge relief when my work capacity started increasing, and that it happened relatively quickly. I wanted to share this with you so that you can feel hopeful about your progress.

Your concentration will improve, but there is another way in which you can increase your efficiency without having to work any harder. Decide, with every piece of written source material, whether you are going to make notes on it or whether you can simply photocopy it from a hard copy source or print it out from an electronic source. This is a simple choice, an apparently minor decision to be made, but it could save you hours. If you need to read, digest and analyse material, then you will want to make notes on it, incorporating not just your understanding of what you are seeing but also your analysis of it. If you are just mining for a few facts, then you could as effectively print or copy the source and use a highlighter pen to point out the salient facts.

Top Tip

Some writers prefer to take this one stage further and, focusing only on the sentences or sections they have highlighted, make a few notes – sometimes just a list of keywords – to help condense the material still further. This is still a speedier process than making notes without first highlighting.

There is a further method you could try which could, again, improve the productivity of this stage of the process. A mass of handwritten notes, or highlighted print outs, will only take you so far. This might, of course, be as far as you want to go when you are taking the first steps in preparing for your report or dissertation: you would not want to impose an artificial structure on your material too early. However, if you are making notes at the point at which you have a rough plan in place, or a fairly firm set of research questions you have set for yourself and your reader, you could impose some order on your notes.

I am not recommending here that you try to write any part of your report or dissertation, even in draft form, but that you could attach a cover sheet to each set of notes or print outs on which you could add some 'surface points'. This could be no more than a bullet pointed list like this:

- Altitude effect – in introduction?
- Steel degradation in girders – must include this – maybe an appendix?

- Cost of steel in China – only relevant until September – recheck before including.
- Design ideas around Millennium Bridge in London – Chapter One. KEY IDEA.

You can then put that set of notes into a plastic wallet ready to be filed away, knowing that there is nothing more you need do to it for now. You will be so pleased, when you come back to the notes later in the process, that you not only made efficient notes, but that you also gave yourself some clues as to where to use them.

Top Tip

It can be a struggle to move away from the reading and research stage into the writing phase; by putting these 'surface points' onto each set of your notes you are deterring yourself from deviating back into any of the source material except the part which you have clearly defined as being of relevance to the section which you are actually working on at that moment.

Know when to stop

This might seem like a strange guideline to have to follow, but consider for a moment the points at which different writers might feel able to stop taking notes from a book:

- When they have checked the division of material in the book to see whether there are any ideas about the presentation of their own data which could be noted in their research notebooks.
- When they have checked the table of contents and decided that the book is not for them.
- When they have checked the table of contents and the 'bibliography', 'references' and/ or 'further reading' sections to see if there are any references they should add to their reading notebooks.
- When they have looked at the table of contents, the bibliography and the index, just to make notes on the few pages (or paragraphs) which are of relevance to them.
- When they have read and absorbed the information in an entire chapter, making notes as they go.
- When they have made notes on a chapter and added a list of surface points to their notes.
- When they have worked through a chapter and checked out all the other chapters by skim reading them, just in case.
- When they have worked through the entire book, on the basis that anything might be relevant, made copious notes and coupled them with a lengthy list of surface points.

I offer you this list (which could be far more extensive – there are so many options) not because I am advocating any of these as the correct way to do things, but to show you that the process of stopping is a complicated one. Any of these could be the right approach, depending on the material you are examining and your purpose in doing so.

As you consider what to do with source material, think back to the five categories for reading material outlined earlier in this chapter. This will give you a clue as to the general approach you will take to the material in front of you. If, on top of this, you are clear about where you want to go with the material, you should be in an excellent position to stop at the best point.

Top Tip

If you are not used to making notes, or it has been some time since you have had to do it, you could return to this section after your first few note-taking sessions. In retrospect, did you stick to each of these three principles, or did you struggle with any of them? By reminding yourself each time of what you are trying to achieve in terms of your note-taking techniques you will find yourself improving markedly and reducing the time you need to set aside for this stage of the process.

Avoid plagiarism

The need to avoid claiming someone else's work, or their research output, or their material, or their ideas, as your own is instinctive in most people, once they have had a chance to think about it. However, knowing exactly what would count as plagiarism and then taking steps to avoid it is not always achieved just by having the right instinct.

- It makes sense to us all that, if you read about someone's research into the potentially beneficial effects of eating blueberries for sufferers of arthritis, and you then quote their data in your own study into the use of redcurrants to do something similar, you need to reference that data back to its source in order to avoid plagiarism.
- What if you simply refer to the fact that this benefit of blueberry consumption has been shown, but do not quote the data or written words of the researcher directly? You probably had no problem deciding on that case: you would still need to reference your source.
- Perhaps you read next about an idea – why not look at the benefits of white currants in this context? You paraphrase the page on which reasons were given for this possible research project. Again, even though you are not quoting directly, you are referring to someone else's published work and you must reference it.
- The fact that blueberries are thought to have all sorts of benefits is well known; they are referred to as a 'superfood' all over the media. If you wanted to begin a document with

the assertion 'Blueberries are commonly heralded as a superfood nowadays: this report/dissertation will test this assertion', you would not need to reference a specific source for your assertion, given that you are claiming it to be common knowledge.

Top Tip

This can be a surprisingly tricky line to draw. If you are immersed in your field it can be easy to overlook the fact that others do not share your knowledge and so you make a generalisation and your readers want a reference, either because they are concerned that you are plagiarising, or because they are unwilling to believe you without proof. It helps to ask a non-specialist 'critical friend' to read through your finished document to check that you have not fallen into this trap.

Even if you feel sure of the ground beneath your feet in the instances offered above, what about the less clear situations?

- If someone says publicly, on a conference platform, that they have found that blueberry consumption can reduce the symptoms of arthritis, but the research is not yet written up and published, would you be plagiarising them if you then went on to make this assertion as a preface to introducing your work on redcurrants?
- What about if that person mentioned this research over coffee at the conference, just to you and in passing?
- Or perhaps you were in an internet chat room and it was mentioned? Or someone tweeted it?

In all of these cases I would either refer to the instance directly or go back to the originator and ask whether the material had been published in a more readily referenced source elsewhere. There is often a lack of clarity about plagiarism and its boundaries, but I have found a golden rule which has ensured that I am never troubled by it: *if you are in any doubt at all, reference your source.*

This rule works so well because, if your reader has no interest in looking at the source, he or she will simply skip over it in the footnotes or not bother to check it out in endnotes. This will never be a problem and will not break the flow of reading, but if a reader does want to check your source, it will always be there.

Top Tip

The reason I used blueberries as the example here is that my daughter mentioned to me earlier that she had heard this on the news. The idea was freely given and so perhaps I would not need to be too concerned about referencing her in this way, but can I trust that my daughter heard correctly? That she remembered the news items in all its details? That she did not, perhaps, mean blackberries when she talked to me about blueberries? This instance demonstrates a significant, but often overlooked, benefit of scrupulously referencing your sources: sometimes other people get it wrong. Now that I have told you that she gave me the idea there is no possibility of me stealing anyone's intellectual property and, if the facts are wrong, you will know who is to blame.

Having established the ways in which plagiarism can occur and agreed upon the need to avoid it, we can move on to some safeguards:

- Find out if your institution or organisation has a set of guidelines on referencing sources. This will give you a good basis on which to write with confidence, always remembering my golden rule if the guidelines leave you in any doubt about a situation.
- Use the internet as if it were a printed source. It may not always be as reliable as most printed, peer-reviewed sources, but nevertheless you need to reference the address (URL) of the page to which you are referring. Given that the internet is an ephemeral medium, and pages can be altered at any time, it can help to print off a page if it contains information which is absolutely vital. That way you do at least have hard-copy evidence. If you want to guarantee accuracy and reliability, you may want to check back to a printed copy of the source material, although of course this is not always possible.
- Record the details of any source on which you are making notes, even if you are unsure about whether you will be using those notes in your final document. That way, you have all the details to hand if you find that you need them. Computer software can help you organise this material, or you can store them in you reading notebook in the first instance.
- An informal reference is better than none. If you have to include a reference to a conversation at a conference because no reference is yet available in print, then do it.

Although my golden rule has kept me from plagiarism problems, it did not help me to overcome another difficulty I encountered in my early days of writing: that of knowing when an idea is, actually, your own. There are times when you are sitting in a lecture or a meeting and taking notes, or making notes as you go through some source material, and you are suddenly struck by the most brilliant idea. Naturally, you note it down as soon as it strikes you, but then your mind is called back to the situation of the moment.

Some days or weeks later, when you come across a rather random 'note to self' like this, it is sometimes impossible to remember: was this your brilliant idea or someone else's genius? You do not want to plagiarise, so you might ignore the idea altogether, but if it is so brilliant that you run with it, convincingly yourself that it really must have been your idea, you will always feel slightly uneasy about it. It took me a long time to find a simple solution. I got into the habit of writing 'my idea' in the margin beside any notes like this. If I go back to my notes on a topic now, even if I wrote them years ago, I can always differentiate between my bright ideas and those of others, which is a great relief.

Top Tip

Self-plagiarism can be as big a problem as regular plagiarism if you are producing an academic document which is being assessed. This term refers to an instance where a writer has already been credited for an output and then tries to gain credit a second time, either on the same course/module or on another. It is also sometimes called 'overlap' or 'double credit'. The rules about this vary from place to place and are sometimes hugely complicated so make sure you are absolutely clear about what you can and cannot use, and if you are in any doubt at all, ask for written clarification.

The idea of self-plagiarism brings us neatly to consider the broader aspects of your 'writing self', how you can identify this part of your intellect and develop it to best effect.

10

Finding your voice

At first thought it might sound a bit highbrow to suggest that you should 'find your voice'; you might come up with the response that you are not planning to be a great author or a poet, and so do not need to find a voice which is unique to you and with which you can engage and inspire others. Except that this is exactly what you are about to do, whether you realise it yet or not. You will be spending many hours deciding on the right material to include in your work: this is the unique basis for your own voice; you will then plan to create an argument, which will allow you to use your original voice; you will write up your work, which will rely on your voice; finally, you will edit and polish your work so as to ensure that your voice is persuasive, consistent and impressive.

So, what is this 'voice' I am talking about? It is a culmination of all the stages I have just described; it is the way in which you say what you have to say: the material you include, the way you lay it out, what you choose to leave out and how you structure an argument all rest upon the fact that, ultimately, you can confidently use the voice of your 'writing self' to engage your reader.

Top Tip

In this chapter we are working together on the broad strokes of your voice. If you have concerns about the detail of how you write, there is help at hand in a later chapter of this guide when we will focus down on the minutiae of writing.

If this is all starting to sound a little daunting, let me reassure you straight away that you already have a 'writing voice'. All of the work we are doing together in this guide is designed to support that voice, to give you the best chance to speak out in a way that is authentic to you. This takes a little work, but it is one of the most rewarding aspects of the task ahead of you. As we work through this chapter I will try to answer the questions you might have and also, where I can, use examples from my own writing style in this guide.

What is my voice now?

It might seem odd to think that you have your own writing voice already, but if you consider it for a few moments you will see that this must be the case. The way you structure your writing, through sentence and paragraph length, is a choice you make instinctively, but you have developed that instinct over time. Similarly, the words you tend to use are your own, and will probably be habitual. I, for example, tend to soften things as I type. Looking back to the previous paragraph I notice that I have used the word 'little' twice, because I would worry that you might be made anxious if this was more than a 'little daunting' and that you would find it too onerous to face more than a 'little work'.

It is not considered to be particularly good style to repeat words like this and so I often find myself going back through my writing and either 'firming up' a paragraph by taking out words like 'little', 'perhaps', 'slightly' and so on. I have not tried to eradicate this tendency altogether, because I genuinely want to reassure my reader that what we are attempting here is perfectly possible, but I know that I must curb this tendency a little (and there I go again ...).

My tendency to soften and qualify what I say is in part a response to what I am trying to achieve, but it is also a symptom of my cultural upbringing. If English is your second language, you might find that your writing voice is markedly different from mine. Of course, there are variations across 'British English' too. The regional accent is most obvious in someone's speaking voice, but an echo of it can come across in writing, too, not just in word choice but also in sentence length and how quickly or slowly a person gets to the heart of an argument.

There is no need to stamp out of your writing anything that marks out your natural tendencies or your national origin: you just need to bear them in mind as we move through this chapter. You will also need to consider the peculiarities of your writing which have come with time. Funnily enough, although these develop over time their origins often lie in one incident; a teacher telling you that you use too many commas without explaining further can insidiously nip away at your confidence in how you use them to the point where you abandon commas altogether.

'Peculiarities' are not necessarily a bad thing; indeed, they can add sprit and vigour to your writing as long as you are aware of them and know how to control them. Take the paragraph above as an example. I have used four different types of punctuation: a colon, a full-stop, a comma and a semi-colon. This enthusiastic use of punctuation might be said to be one of my peculiarities but it would not be a problem unless I used so much that my sentences become impenetrable. Another one of my peculiarities is something that you will not see here: the use of a dash – like this one. I was told many years ago that this was too casual a mark to be used in formal writing and so I tend to avoid it and use a colon in its place. Again, this is not a problem, but the final peculiarity I am going to share with you might be …

I do not contract my words. You will not find in this guide the use of 'won't', 'couldn't', 'we'll', 'you've' and such like (although there are two 'let's' in here, because they were the best of several evils in making sentences I needed to use flow well). For my taste this is too informal for a guide such as this. As I am advocating care and precision in your writing I want to offer you the same courtesy and take care that my writing is friendly but still formal and precise. However, another writer might feel equally strongly that a more casual style of writing is appropriate in a context such as this. Add to this the fact that you already have a 'writing voice', which might be formal or could equally well be very casual, and you can see that you have some decisions to make.

In that last paragraph the idea of feeling strongly about something is the thought I want you to take from here. Writing in a style appropriate to the setting, whatever you deem that style to be, is what we are aiming for. You, too, need to feel strongly that you are using the best voice for the circumstances; the only time writers have a problem with this is if they have not thought about it. In a report or a dissertation you are most likely to want to maintain a formal, professional register and so this is where you need to aim.

Top Tip

It is no coincidence that the word register (used here to mean, in effect, the level of formality you introduce into your writing style) is the same word used to describe the register of a speaking voice (that is, whether it is a high or low voice). Reading is very similar in this respect to listening to someone: the reader cannot help but make some instant decisions about the writer and you want all of these to be positive. Your register shows that you care and that you want to connect with the reader. Ask a friend or colleague to read some of your writing with only this in mind: what first impression are you giving?

Do I need an elevated voice?

If you are to suit your voice to your purpose you need to recognise the strengths in your writing and add to them whilst simultaneously eradicating bad habits and weaknesses. However, context is all important in this. Although you will need an elevated voice in a report or dissertation, one that commands respect and persuades your reader, this does not mean that you would write in this style in all situations.

In an email, for example, my writing style would differ from my voice in this book. I would contract my words, I would happily use abbreviations and there would be dashes everywhere. This would be fine if I were chatting with a colleague; in fact, it would be more than fine. If I were to receive an email which began with 'Dear Dr Becker' from a colleague with whom I had been chatting on first name terms earlier in the day, I would be taken aback. If the tone of the email were overly formal then I might think that colleague to be pompous and distant; I would be less likely to want to give them whatever they asked for in the email. You can see from this brief example that your challenge is not to elevate your style of writing on every occasion, or to adopt a formal or professional register for each document, but rather to suit your writing to the occasion by thinking of both the person you want to be in that situation and the needs and expectations of your readers.

Over time, your writing voice will become responsive and flexible, offering you a palette of styles and nuances from which you will choose with little conscious effort. For now, it will take a little more effort. To keep you motivated as you work on this, here are some returns you can expect to gain if you can find the right voice:

1. It will increase the sense of occasion in your writing. If I read a document which is well written, I feel drawn to give it more attention. It also makes it much easier to read, which would naturally incline an assessor to award it a higher mark if it were an assessed dissertation.
2. Writing with a professional voice shows that you care enough to take the trouble to make this document the best it can be. My response would be to accord it more respect: if you have taken the trouble to produce an elegant and persuasive report, I will be inclined to listen more carefully to what you have to say.
3. It is easier to work within a word count if you can control your writing voice. You will be able to make yourself a touch more succinct or more persuasively articulate without any great effort. If you do go a fraction over or under on the word count, fixing it will be easy as you will be able to see relatively easily where you were too verbose or the point where you could improve the piece by writing in a slightly more expansive style.

4. Your writing must support your argument, otherwise the other work you are doing here, all of the information gathering and sorting, the planning and the polishing, will be wasted. You want to achieve a goal and present an overarching argument; when you have command of your writing voice you will find that you can focus on the detail of what you are writing without losing sight of these.

What will affect the writing voice I use?

Several aspects of the situation will come into play here:

1. **The context**: Is this an assessed piece of work? Is it sole- or joint-authored? Is the setting professional or more social or collegiate? Are you a leader or a team player in this context? How familiar are you with the topic area? Are you seen as expert?
2. **The form**: A report will be more formal than an email; a specification would follow very formal lines and carry its own version of a professional voice; a business case or tender document would be impressive and persuasive; a dissertation would be flowing and yet well structured.
3. **The reader**: This is absolutely crucial. Are there several intended readers? Do they know you? Will they know in advance what you are trying to do? Will they have been involved in a project or research activity with you?
4. **Your aims**: You might be producing work to be formally assessed in an academic or professional setting; you might be seeking to persuade the reader to offer you more funding or to respond positively to a set of recommendations; you might simply be giving information in the most authoritative way possible. Whatever you are trying to do, you will always be trying to persuade somebody of something: this simple fact should never be forgotten by any writer.
5. **What sort of person are you trying to be?** Although this is not always a helpful approach because it can distract you from your aim of writing fluently, some writers do find it useful to think about the sort of person they would like their readers to think them to be.

Top Tip

If you would like to try out this last approach there are several 'tricks' you might try. Some writers put a photo of themselves looking serious/friendly/professional/smiling or whatever on the wall in front of them as they write. Others put a generic picture of their ideal reader in front of them – just a snapshot from the internet of a smiling student, for example. Some even go so far as to dress appropriately for the occasion. I know one writer who simply cannot face writing when wearing a suit jacket; I know another who always wears high heels at the computer. All of these tricks work for those writers, so it is not too far-fetched to suggest that you set yourself up in such a way as to remind you of your writing persona and your target reader.

How can I elevate my style?

I hope by now that you are convinced about the need to be able to find several writing voices and to use them in a way that is appropriate to the context; I hope also that you are reassured that this will come with time to some extent and so should not make you unduly anxious. Despite this, I would like to offer you some ways in which you can get ahead on this aspect of your writing development. In the context of reports and dissertations, your style is unlikely to be anything other than elevated. That is, relatively formal, always well informed, persuasive and controlled but accessible.

Achieving that long list of accomplishments does not start, as you might expect, with writing anything at all, but rather through your reading. You need to immerse yourself in your topic area. Alternate between more challenging reading and working through material in your field which you find easier to absorb. All the time you will be assimilating the language or your field almost without noticing. In this respect it is best to read a little in your topic area every day rather than spending hours reading on just one day of the week.

I have just suggested that you will be assimilating the language 'almost without realising'. I did this because I would like to recommend that, every now and then as you carry out your research, you do consciously consider the nature of the writing that you are reading. You need not work too hard here, or take notes on how something is being written, but make an effort to notice if the sentences tend to be long or short, whether the paragraphs are dense or easy to manage, whether there are any words which you keep coming across and which you might like to use. You will not feel as if you are making any great effort in doing this, but it will have a positive effect in helping you to adopt the language, style and tone of your chosen field.

Top Tip

The technique I have described here is also useful if you have trouble with your spelling, especially if you were once adept at spelling but suspect that spellcheck has weakened your spelling ability. Just making this effort to notice, even every few days, can help to improve your spelling surprisingly quickly.

Reading will only take you so far. We retain facts more easily if we put them to use and the same principle applies to your writing style. You need to write regularly so that what you are assimilating can flow out of the end of your fingertips, onto the keyboard (or through pen to paper) and so reinforce the development of your writing style. What you write will need to be in your topic area for this process to work at its best, but it need not be part of your report or dissertation, even in draft. Indeed, I would caution against writing draft after draft of your output unless you are certain that this approach works for you.

When I wrote about making notes in the last chapter you may recall that I suggested making 'surface notes' so that your work becomes more focused, allowing you in effect to create a reference guide to each set of notes you produce, ready for when you come to write your dissertation or report. It is to these surface notes that you could turn now in your effort to elevate your style. The detailed notes you make on your source material will often be rather disjointed, probably with some crossings out and some random notes to yourself to check out new areas of thought. They will not hang together as continuous prose, nor should they. You would not want to interrupt your successful note-taking approach in order to work on your writing style, but you could deliberately elevate your style when writing your surface notes. In addition to a bullet pointed list of the main points, and a few suggestions of how this material and your analysis might fit into your final output, you could try writing a few sentences which summarise all that you have noted from that source. The point would not be to produce the perfect synopsis in all respects, but rather to keep writing, working on your style and reinforcing the elevation of style which you are noticing in your reading.

Top Tip

My doctoral supervisor gave me two pieces of advice when I began my PhD research: assume that none of your early plans will work quite as well as you expect (I wrote from my seventh full plan) and never, ever stop writing, even if you are only writing notes, drafts or a synopsis of the material covered in a day (she was right, I have never stopped).

The fact that much of the work on your writing style actually happens before you write your report or dissertation is to your advantage, allowing your style to develop in a natural way and giving you the chance to experiment with a variety of techniques. However, there is also work to do once you have finished writing. All of us are likely to produce some variations in style if we are composing an extended piece of writing; this is only natural. You will be writing at different times of day, you will be interrupted from time to time, you will have to take breaks now and then, and there will be times when you feel more confidence in what you are saying than at other times.

None of this can be avoided easily and there is no great need to do so; it is far easier to smooth out your tone and style at the proofreading stage. It is for this reason that I would urge you to proofread relatively soon after completing the document: leaving it alone for several weeks will be counterproductive. You are probably already aware that it is good practice to leave your writing to one side for a while once it is complete so as to remove yourself mentally from the work. This helps you to spot mistakes and style variations more easily. However, if you leave the work aside for so long that you forget how it felt to write it, you might also lose the detailed sense of purpose that came with that. Similarly, if you have not read or written anything in that field for some weeks, you might already be losing your familiarity with your writing voice in that arena. So, take a decent break between writing and checking and then keep in mind that you are looking for more than mistakes: you are trying to ensure that your voice is authentic and persuasive throughout.

What could get in the way of my developing voice?

Once you have developed a writing voice you will become ever more sure of it, confident that it really is your voice (or, more accurately, one of the voices at your disposal) and that you will be able to command it without difficulty. However, this will take time. You can make positive changes to your writing voices over just a few weeks, but it can take months and years to develop it fully.

Although you can look to your writing future with great confidence, in the shorter term it is natural to be knocked off course every now and then. This will not matter on a practical level – you can rewrite a paragraph or two easily enough – but it can be unnerving, so watch out for the three most common triggers for 'losing your voice':

1. **Nerves**: If you are especially nervous, your writing might become overcomplicated (using unusually long words when simple words would do) or pompous in tone or clichéd (in particular by including redundant phrases repeatedly). If you notice that your writing style is dipping, take a moment and check back to your plan. Satisfy yourself that there is no real reason to be nervous (you have all the evidence, your argument hangs together, your knowledge is sound) and, once you are convinced that there is no problem beyond a momentary attack of nerves, go back to writing.
2. **Observers**: If you are writing alongside others (your fellow students producing their dissertations or project reports at the same time; your colleagues also producing reports for the client), it is easy to listen to 'helpful' advice which is often little more than a series of random opinions, or shared scare stories about writing problems. This holds true for face-to-face conversations and those online. If you are finding the voices of others looming too large in your mind as you write, take the time to change the situation so that you can write undisturbed and without commentators.

3. Timing: If you are under too much (or, interestingly, too little) time pressure, you might struggle to find the right voice for the document. Sounding unfocused, or nervous, or stressed, will never make for a convincing writing voice. The organising and planning techniques offered throughout this guide will help to keep you working within the time-frame you have been given.

How will I know when I am there?

Some writers rely on circulating drafts of early versions of their work so as to get feedback not just on the content, but also on the style. This can be useful if you welcome feedback and have friends and supporters who are able to comment on this aspect of your writing with confidence and without simply trying to impose their writing style on your work. Treat this option with caution until you know that it works well for you.

All of the work you will be doing to appropriate a voice which suits your purpose, and then to make that style uniquely your own, will only be worthwhile if you are able to recognise when you have reached your goal. Of course, the idea of 'perfect writing' is a fallacy. There will always be work to do, but you will reach a plateau where you are tinkering with the odd infelicity of phrase or awkward tone of writing voice rather than feeling lost in a choppy sea of different styles.

As you might expect, I have spent decades pondering over writing, my own and others', and even now I have moments when I read something I have written and wonder what on earth I was thinking. It happens to all of us and it will happen to you, too, despite your efforts, but these moments will occur less frequently and you will come to a point where they are idly amusing rather momentarily devastating. There will often be people around you whose job it is to comment on your writing: your dissertation supervisor and assessors, your colleagues and your boss, your clients and your critics. Beyond this, I have come to realise that there is one infallible way to know when you have found the right voice: when people stop noticing your style and just take notice of what you have to say.

PART THREE
Planning

Meticulous planning is the cornerstone of effective writing, but only if you use a planning method which matches well with the way your mind works and suits the type of document you are producing. The work you do in this part can be applied not just to planning a document, but also to organising a project or bringing your research tasks under control.

In this part I am going to be looking at the challenges of planning your report or dissertation and I will be focusing on the stages when you will be pulling together material and trying to order it so as to create a persuasive and successful document. However, we should not overlook the length of additional preparation time involved in producing a report (sometimes weeks or months) or a dissertation (sometimes a year, or even more). With this in mind, you might want to produce a timeline or timetable at the very outset, showing how much time you have to think through the task, to scout around for material, to plan an initial argument, to gather and categorise material, and to discuss and refine your arguments, all of which will happen before you reach the writing-up stage.

11

Are you a natural planner?

We need to consider this question even before we begin to think about how you might plan your dissertation or report, because the answer will have a direct influence on how you work from this point onwards. If you are a natural planner, you will not find this chapter too challenging, you will happily work your way through it and then you will probably devise your own method of planning, based to some extent on my suggestions here. If you are not a natural planner, you may find this chapter less appealing in prospect, but once you have mastered a planning method you will be pleased to have it in your writing tool box and you are unlikely to deviate much from that method.

I am going to describe a few situations from which you can gain clues as to whether or not you are a natural planner:

1. You are going on holiday. You know where you are going to be staying every night; you have a list of roughly what you would like to do each day. In fact, you relish planning the holiday almost as much as (if not more than) you enjoy going on the holiday.
2. It is Friday lunchtime. You already know what you want to achieve over the weekend. Indeed, you have a list ready to go so that you can tick things off it throughout the weekend to make sure that you get everything done.
3. You are about to go food shopping. Everything that you need is on a list (either on paper or in your head) and you will walk around the shop in a methodical fashion picking up your groceries. Everything on your list will end up in your trolley, but not much else.
4. You enjoy lists and you love the 'sticky notes' program on your computer, so that you can build a list on your screen. When you make a list you deliberately include some easy tasks (or even some tasks which you have already almost completed) just for the satisfaction of getting an 'easy tick' on your list.

If any of these situations sounds like your day-to-day life, you are probably a natural planner. Most natural planners tend to know this about themselves, but if you are not sure it is worth noting that appearances can be deceptive in identifying planners. Those who are not natural planners might make lots of lists, and so look like planners, but they do not enjoy the lists much and might tend to forget to look at them once their good resolution wears off. On the other hand, natural planners might not make lists at all, not because they do not enjoy them, but because they are so organised that they naturally compartmentalise and list things in their minds to such an extent that they do not need to write them down.

Top Tip

Those whose minds are naturally very organised will sometimes say that they plan just by jotting down a list of headings and working from there. Those who are not natural planners will sometimes get everything down on paper and then try to order the material by cutting and pasting or rewriting. Although these approaches can work in some circumstances, they can also cause you problems and be far too time consuming, so if you usually take either of these approaches, read on …

Is there a 'best' way to be?

The simple answer to this is 'no', and I can demonstrate why. I am sometimes asked to produce teaching material alongside a colleague of mine, usually for a new module, and these tend to be discussed and agreed several months before they will be taught. I am a natural planner and he is not. As I leave the meeting in which we have decided with our colleagues to produce a new degree module, I am already planning what areas we might cover; by the time I have reached my office I have a snappy title for the module; over the next few days I rough out a module outline and begin to make a draft allocation of the teaching of the module.

Within a week or so I will have set up a virtual learning environment online and begun to populate the site with useful information. All the time I am doing this, my colleague is apparently doing nothing. Absolutely nothing at all. When we meet in the coffee room or in meetings I will casually ask how he is getting on with the new module and he looks momentarily confused before appearing to remember the module and then offering platitudes such as 'plenty of time yet' or, nearer the start of term, earnest assurances of 'yes, I must get on with that'. As a natural planner this, of course, is driving me around the bend with frustration.

I persevere and, the week before the module is due to begin, I remind my colleague by email that I asked him to look at the online material, that I sent him the module outline some months ago and that we need to ask colleagues, now as a matter of some urgency, if they can lecture on the module. By this time I am usually promising myself never to work with the man again: until he replies. Under the impetus of mounting urgency, he has checked through my module outline and discovered that, in my rush to get things done efficiently, I have overlooked a vital component of the module.

It turns out that, although he has not formally asked anyone to lecture on the module, he has been mentioning it to people for months and so has no trouble lining up lecturers for the entire module. He has not bothered to look at the online material, but when he does (the night before the module starts) he is able to contribute some thoughtful and supportive material. When we stand together to address the group of students on the module for the first time, I am frazzled from having chased him for months; he cannot understand what the fuss is about.

So why do I persist? Because I know that he will find the cracks in my planning, seeing the important points that I have missed in my hurry and offering well thought-out advice and material. Similarly, he works with me because he knows that in that first lecture I will know exactly where to go, I will have an attendance register to hand and I will know the names of all the students. One way is not better than the other, it is just different, and our task in life is often to recognise 'our way' and then try to compensate for the disadvantages of this way whilst maximising its advantages.

In terms of a report or dissertation, you will find it helpful to consider at this early stage whether you are a natural planner or not. That way, you will recognise the best way to work for you. Thinking back to earlier sections of this book, it will not come as a surprise to know that the 'fast and frantic' writer tends not to be the natural planner, whilst the 'steady and controlled' writer usually is a natural planner.

So why should I plan?

This is a good question. I have just suggested to you that natural planners can often plan in their heads rather than on a piece of paper, and that those who are not natural planners tend to forget to look at plans, so the case for planning might seem rather hopeless. It is, nevertheless, still important to plan, and there are several reasons for this:

1. Most of us, even if we do not consciously note it, can spot an unplanned report or dissertation without any trouble at all. For those of us who assess dissertations and reports, we can see that the work just does not quite knit together. There is a change of emphasis where one would not expect it, or an argument is introduced without being further developed, or the supporting material for an argument seems uneven.

Even for those readers not assessing a lengthy document, they will instinctively respond differently to a document which has not been planned in advance of writing. Although all of the material could be there, it will not flow as well as it might, the register of the writing voice will fluctuate and the argument will seem unstable at times. This will distract and unsettle the reader.

Top Tip

The best sort of writing is that where a reader does not have to think too much about the process of writing which went into the document. You will want your own writing style, of course, and you will want the reader to respond to that style, but you will not want a reader who is confused by inconsistencies of structure or writing.

2. However straightforward a document might seem in prospect, it can grow in complexity at an alarming rate as your understanding of the situation increases and your ideas proliferate. A plan ensures that this will not cause you too many problems.

Top Tip

Even if I have planned a document out using a brief, bullet-pointed list or a series of main headings, I would still revert to a more comprehensive planning method, such as a spider chart, as soon as I had an inkling that things were about to get more complicated.

3. Although your thoughts can be in perfect formation at the outset of a project, over time your recollection of what you intended to do can lose some of its clarity. If you are working on a project over many months it can be disconcerting to find that you are losing your way just because you did not make a full enough plan to capture all of your ideas and intentions.

Top Tip

If you produce a series of plans over time, which you may well do in a lengthy project as your ideas develop, it can be handy to date each of your plans. That way you can look back at your progress more easily: this can be a great confidence boost.

4. If you find that you have to reduce the length of a report or dissertation in the planning stages, or you realise that you are not going to be able to keep to the word count if you write down everything you would like to cover, it is far easier to lop off and discard one section of a plan than it is to delete a whole section of a written document and then try to cover over the breaks.

Top Tip

If you know that losing anything from your plan would be stressful for you, remember that it need not be lost. If you plan meticulously you will be able to file away the discarded section of the plan, knowing that it is ready for future use if you return to this topic area in another project.

5. Life gets busy. However firm your intentions, you might be taken away from your project for days or weeks at a time, perhaps without prior warning. A good plan will secure your thoughts, which will in turn reduce your level of stress at having to abandon a project for a time.

Top Tip

In this respect plans are real time savers. By securing everything in a plan, you will be able to come back to your project far more easily; instead of wasting time trying to recall where you were in your thoughts, you can pick up exactly where you left off by just glancing though your plan.

6. Some of us enjoy leading a team; others find it far more onerous. Planning can help cement your team's identity and boost team morale. By asking all members of the team to join with you in planning an overview of your project, you are including each member and encouraging everyone to take responsibility for the success of the project. This is equally true for projects, reports, dissertations and presentations: involvement at the planning stage helps you to communicate with each other and should improve results.

Top Tip

If your project group is geographically scattered, or if some members of the team are not natural team players, it can be useful to ask individual team members to produce a detailed draft plan of just one section of the project, report or dissertation. That way you know that it will have been considered in detail and that each team member will feel valued. You will, of course, have to explain that not every aspect of their plan will necessarily be included in the final document or project brief.

7. There is another way in which a plan can help you to communicate. If you have been given a report brief which is confusing, or you have decided with your supervisor on a dissertation title without exactly understanding what your supervisor intended you to do, it is fine to go back and ask for clarification. However, if you are still confused after a couple of requests for more information and guidance, it can be embarrassing to ask yet again; it is also unlikely that you will gain any more clarity from asking the same questions repeatedly.

If you find yourself in this situation, use your plan to communicate. Make a plan to the level of detail you feel you can achieve from the information you have been given, and then go along to your manager or your supervisor and hold the plan up with the simple question 'is this what you think I am going to be producing?'. You might be amazed at how positive this experience can be. Most people find it far easier to say that you are on the wrong track and to show you what they mean if they have your plan in front of them. It is simple enough to take out a red pen and cross out a whole section of plan, and far easier than trying to describe what is needed over and over again.

Top Tip

If you find yourself unnerved by the very thought of approaching your boss or your supervisor with such a bold question, or if you are embarrassed because you think that you should have understood the instructions by now, you can always scan your plan and send it via email.

8. Plans, once you get into the habit of producing them, can be tremendously reassuring. By laying everything out on paper you can more easily see if you have left out a whole section of material which should be included, you can spot holes in your argument and you can identify illogical progression with ease. It is this pleasing sense of taking control and being supported by a plan which is the greatest draw to planning for many writers.

Top Tip

Returning for a moment to the example I gave above of my colleague. It took me several years to devise a solution to this problematic situation. Just this year I decided on the best way for us to work together. I hold back on my enthusiasm for getting on with things just long enough to send him my rough plans for a module outline and my more detailed plans for the website material before I go any further. Because these plans are less over-whelming than the finished article, he is happy to make a concession to my approach by looking at the plans much earlier and pointing out to me my inevitable oversights and errors.

12

A planning strategy

As well as committing to the idea of making a plan at all, you could benefit from devising a strategy for planning; that is, deciding when and at what level to plan at each point in the process.

Preparing to plan

For most of us the best way to plan is without any interruptions at all except those that we make for ourselves. This means, ideally, planning away from the hustle and bustle of work or your usual, crowded study area and sitting alone to think through a plan.

 **Top Tip**

Being uninterrupted does not necessarily mean working silently. Some writers prefer to work with a radio on in the background or music quietly playing though their headphones. If this is the way you usually study or write, it will work equally well for planning.

When to plan

You are likely to make several plans as you move ahead with a project, so you will need to heed the clues as to when you should return to the planning:

1. As soon as you feel you have a good enough grasp of your overall purpose, make the initial six-point plan descried in the next chapter. This could be within minutes of getting a report brief or agreeing to a dissertation title. Force yourself to do this even if you feel little inclination to plan at such an early stage: it will save you time later.

2. Only make a draft overview plan (your first spider chart, for example) when you feel that a picture of the whole document is emerging. Remind yourself that this need not be your final plan and so you can be free flowing in your approach.

3. Produce a revised plan, or section of a plan, at each point where you find new research questions which you feel could alter the course of your project. Again, you are not committing to these ideas being included in the final document, but rather trying them out to see what impact they would have on your overarching argument.

4. If you become anxious, feeling that you are losing sight of where you are going, return to your last plan and remind yourself of your goal; this might also be a good moment to revise it in the light of your recent material gathering.

5. If you are concerned that the project is becoming unwieldy and that as a result you might produce an unfocused report or go over your dissertation word count, do not go back to your last plan but instead make a new plan from memory, only noting down the most important points you expect to be covering. You might have remembered your plan perfectly to the last detail, but if you did miss anything out, that might be the area which you could sensibly discard without damaging the piece overall.

6. If you are working with your manager, mentor or supervisor in developing your ideas, producing a revised plan together each time you meet can be very productive.

7. In addition to your overview plan, which will become more detailed and firmer over time, you may want to produce separate plans for each chapter or section of your report or dissertation. This level of detail can be reassuring once you come to write and moving away from your overview plan to a smaller plan can be a relief as it will be more easily manageable.

Top Tip

There is one point at which I would urge you *not* to make a new plan, and that is once you have begun to write. By that stage you should have a plan in place which is firm enough and has sufficient detail from which to write. The only exception to this would be if you had produced no more than an outline plan of a section or chapter, in which case it might make sense to produce a fuller plan before you embark on that piece of the whole.

When to stop planning

Having offered you so many instances of when you might make or revise your plans, one obvious question you might ask is 'when do I actually get to write anything?'. When can you be sure that you can write with confidence, that you have reached a point whereby that is the only next logical step? Sadly, this question can only have the rather vague answer 'when you feel ready'. This is not enough, so let me try to make it clearer.

Planning is where the truly hard work of writing a report or dissertation takes place. In the phases before that you are gathering material and analysing it, seeing how it might fit into your argument and trying to get to grips with the research questions it throws up. This is not easy, of course, but it carries relatively little responsibility. You are free to range across a field of material, stopping along the way to dive into any material which interests you particularly and with only a light-touch obligation to bear in mind that it will have to be organised at some stage: your surface notes will be doing this work as you go along.

In the stages after the planning you will be writing, and this should be the equivalent of a ski slope down which you will be whizzing with confidence. You will look up regularly, to make sure that your style is good, you might occasionally slalom to one side or another as you nuance your argument a little more, at times you might pause in your descent to look around at what you are achieving, but generally you are on a clearly defined path down the mountain.

After the writing you will have the pleasure (and I will show you how to make it a genuine pleasure) of editing, polishing and proofing your work. So, if the hard work lies principally with the planning, how do you know when you can stop? There will be signs:

- When you instinctively feel that you cannot be clearer about your overall argument.
- When you have an urge to communicate with your reader.
- When you stop dreading the writing and start to feel a real need to get on with it, not to get the task out of the way but because you want to convey your message.
- When you find that your planning is becoming counterproductive or repetitive; that the more you plan the more you are complicating things to no great purpose.
- When you are becoming anxious that your topic will become stale and boring unless you write it up.

Top Tip

If you have spotted some or all of these clues and yet you are nervous about starting to write in case you have not planned thoroughly enough, you can test yourself easily enough. If you can write a convincing introduction, and find as you write you do not have to stop repeatedly to check what you want to say or alter your way of saying it, you have done enough.

You will see from this chapter that the phrase 'writing a dissertation or report' is not at all an accurate reflection of what you are doing. The writing is a challenge, of course, but it is one you can meet more easily once you recognise that the other stages of the process, and in particular the planning, are of great importance in getting it right.

13

Your first step

A plan can become detailed and complex as it develops over time and is altered to suit your needs. If it does not perfectly support your argument, you will return to it to interrogate your original hypothesis; if it does not provide enough reassurance, you will make it more detailed until you feel confident of what you are doing; if it seems disjointed or uneven, you will want to revise and smooth it out before you work from it.

Each of these activities will come when you begin to plan in detail, but there is one small task you need to carry out first. It might seem minor, even insignificant, but it will have an impact on your way of thinking about your topic area and, in the later stages of planning, it could save you from making fundamental mistakes. Before you make any detailed plans, you must force yourself to produce an initial six-point list of main areas.

We none of us can remember, or work unaided with, more than about six points. In fact, most of us would prefer four or five. You may not have given this much thought before, but you see it all around you. A major speech will contain no more than six main points to make it easy for the press to report; a good lecture will do the same. (The last political speech I heard reported covered the economy, the UK's position in Europe, the future of the National Health Service and the education systems in the UK and the changes about to be made to the transport infrastructure. These are five huge areas, and I cannot recall every detail I was offered, but I know what that political leader sees as vital areas of concern for the UK in the coming months.) It is not just in speeches or lectures that this happens. The structure of a European play is traditionally five acts, three before the interval and two after. If you have an intellectual argument with someone it might rage for hours, but you will run out of steam rapidly once you have reached your sixth major point.

Top Tip

Next time you attend a meeting where someone is giving a presentation or a talk and is trying to persuade the group to do something, make a conscious note of how many key points are introduced and look around if the speaker reaches point number seven: you will see my case made for me as attention suddenly drops off.

So, you have to face the fact that six main points will need to suffice in order for you to make your argument. Each point may have many sections and subsections, but you have to grasp those six (or four, or five) key points. This might come as a relief to you, if you were wondering how on earth you were going to write so many words on such a relatively narrow topic; it may fill you with horror if you were already wondering how to cope with a complicated area.

The way to find your initial points is to force yourself to list them in a minute or less. At what point in the process you do this is going to be important. If you do it too early, you may find that you cannot think of six points which carry enough weight to provide a sense of where you are going; leave it too late and you risk losing the main points in the mass of material you have acquired. The best way I have found to approach this is to recognise when you are coming to the stage where you can embark on a draft plan and then make your six points just before you begin work on that plan. I would tend to gather material and then plan, others might make a skeleton plan right at the outset: either of these tactics would allow you to work on a six-point plan.

Top Tip

There is no need to worry if your six-point plan is actually a four- or five-point plan: this may accurately reflect the argument you are trying to make. It is only if you find yourself straying beyond seven main points that you need to ask yourself why, and consider whether in fact you are losing your clear overview.

When you make your six-point plan you will have to ambush yourself. That is, try not to plan too far ahead in your mind before you do it. Take a blank sheet of paper and give yourself no more than a minute to write down your absolutely essential, main points. When you contemplate the points they might not yet look to you as if they could hang together as a convincing argument, but they will all be major points which you feel must be included.

When you come to write down your six main points, try to avoid generic words such as 'introduction' (that will always be there) or 'what, when, why?' (these are unlikely to be individual enough). Also avoid words which do not mean much in most contexts, such as 'logistics', or phrases which are so broad as to be encompassing your entire dissertation or report, such as 'how does it work?' or 'make a business case'. Each of the six points must be real and relevant.

Top Tip

The timing here is vital. If you give yourself more than a minute you risk finding 16 points and believing that they will all be main sections in your report or dissertation. It is hard to get back from this position, so make sure that when you are jotting down your six main points you feel slightly hassled, under pressure of time and forced just to get on with it, rather than giving yourself too much time to ponder.

Dyslexia and organisation

Although I am recommending that you artificially induce stress in order to produce your six-point plan, by timing yourself and forcing yourself to write down just these few points, for some writers this would be more than stressful: it would be distressing. If dyslexia is affecting your organisational skills, you might find it especially difficult to narrow down to just a few points, or you might jump in with six points and then change your mind repeatedly.

The six-point plan can be a very difficult task in these circumstances, but it can also be of most benefit to those with dyslexia, as it grounds you in an overview of just six points which, however imperfect, will help keep you to task later if your plan becomes unfocused and difficult to control. On the other hand, if you find it extremely burdensome to try to produce a six-point plan, then this could sap your confidence before you even start to plan more systematically. You know yourself best and so this is a judgement call which can safely be left with you.

Although for all writers it will have been a stressful minute of frantic thought and scribbling, you will end up in the secure position of having a six-point plan, with the sense of reassurance that this brings. Once you have this in hand you might expect to take it with you to the next stage of more detailed planning. In fact, I am going to ask you to set it aside for quite some time. These are unlikely to be the six main points you finally end up using in your report, but they will help to keep you on track. When you have produced your outline plan, and some more detailed plans, look back at your six points if you run out of ideas about the key points to include in the plan; every now and then glance back at them as you work through your detailed planning, just to remind yourself of where you started.

There is one last moment when you will look back at this six-point plan: just before you begin to write. You will by then have a fully formed plan, with all of the detail you need to push off on that downhill ski slope of writing. By looking back at your six points now you will be giving yourself a last chance to change your mind about your plan, maybe to include something you had forgotten about since that first pressurised minute of planning, or perhaps a reordering of your argument so that it is more in line with your original intentions. In most cases you will not make any changes at all, but it will seal your confidence in your plan to go through this little ritual. Now you will be in a position to write; you will feel a little anxious, of course, but this will be overridden by your desire to get on to the next stage of the process.

14

Four planning methods

There are, at least potentially, as many different planning methods as there are people to use them. As soon as somebody picks up a method and uses it, it is open to that writer to make some modifications. Over time, the modifications to one method can become significant enough for somebody to refine it still further and give it a new name, even though its basic working system is fundamentally the same as another method. I intend to work with you through four planning methods which will suffice to give you a range of planning tools from which to choose. With each method I will offer some guidance on the circumstances to which it might be best suited and the way in which it might affect your writing/structuring style.

The four methods I will be exploring with you here are:

- a spider chart
- a flowchart
- a brainstorm
- a mind map.

For each of these I will describe how the method works, talk about how you might use it, and consider its advantages and potential disadvantages.

Top Tip

A word of warning: you can only sensibly use a planning method which suits how you think, and you can only take that method to a level of complexity which works for you. If you try to use a method which does not work with how your brain naturally organises material, you will feel frustrated and confused; if you go beyond the level of detail which works for you, you will be left feeling perhaps less organised than when you started out. As you put these plans into action, be prepared to discard a method and move to another if needed.

The spider chart

This is sometimes called 'a spider diagram' or just 'a spider'. It works especially well if you are trying to create an argument or want to look at several aspects of a situation or problem. Although no planning method will have more than a minor effect on your writing style, that is sometimes all you need. A spider chart lends itself to a discursive style of writing, with longer sentences and paragraphs and, in general, more fluency and expansiveness. Thus a spider chart could be a useful method if you have been writing a series of succinct documents, with a clipped style of writing, and now want to break free into a more fluid style.

There are several stages to creating a spider chart:

1. A spider chart works by drawing a circle at the centre of a piece of paper in which you write down a few key words about your document. This would not be the whole title of your dissertation or report but rather the words which seem to you to carry the essential meaning of that title. So, for example: 'An exploration of the ways in which global warming is affecting the timber trade in Norway' could become:

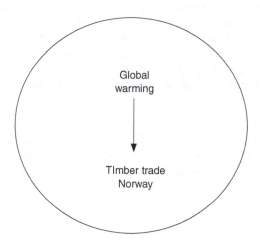

Similarly: 'An analysis of the effect of monetary easing on Gross Domestic Product' could become:

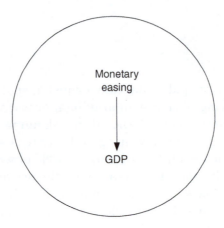

2. The spider chart is then developed on the page, with lines radiating out from the centre (representing the 'legs' of the spider) and additional circles attached to those lines (representing the 'feet' of the spider).

Top Tip

As you develop your spider chart you may well change your mind. This would be perfectly natural and is a productive part of the process. However, some writers find it distracting, even distressing, to produce a spider chart with crossings out all over it; they would rather produce a whole new chart each time they change their mind. If you know that you have this tendency, consider writing down your points on sticky notes; that way you can attach them to your plan and move them about whenever you like without spoiling the neatness of the chart.

In this way, a document with the title 'Shakespeare's *Romeo and Juliet* can be made, with suitable directorial intervention, as relevant to today's audience as it was to Shakespeare's contemporaries' would become, in the next phase of the spider chart, something like this:

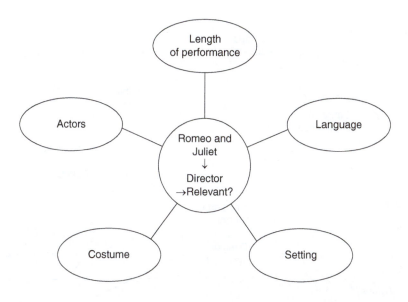

This would provide you with a basic spider chart, but most situations would require a writer to go further than this.

3. The third stage asks that you transmogrify each of the feet of the spider into new, smaller spiders. This is done by making new points around each.

   In the example above, this would mean producing a spider chart with this level of complexity.

Top Tip

Planning effectively is not just about knowing which method to use, it is also about judging how far to push that method. For me, this spider chart would be enough; for others, there would be a further stage of inserting arrows to show connections, or colouring in the feet to aid recall or adding symbols such as + and – to show the development of an argument. It is only by experimenting that you will find out how far you can go without it becoming counterintuitive for you.

A spider chart works well if you are trying to create an argument. Its structure encourages you to keep thinking more widely so as to place the next foot

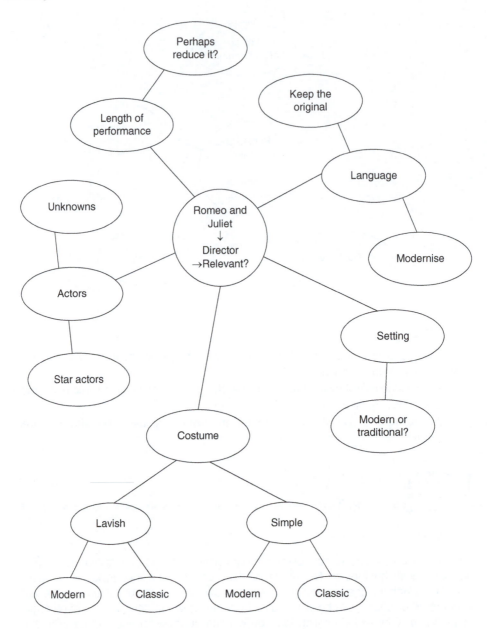

of the spider, whilst ensuring that you never lose your way. Even if you are writing about a far-flung foot which contains the most minor of points in your argument, you will still be aware, because of the connecting lines, that your principal focus is on the title of the work. In a dissertation, a spider chart can help you to contain large amounts of material in a relatively small space. For a report, it can be useful in helping you to number your headings.

The example I have already given could be numbered for a report in this way:

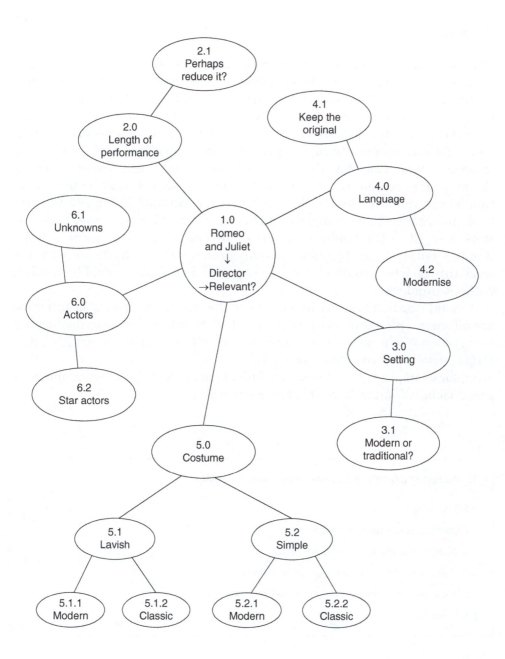

If you are producing a dissertation, it can still be very useful at this stage to number the plan as if for a report, even if you only number the main sections. This way you have a clear view of how your dissertation will be structured before you move on to the next step.

Decimal notation

This is a concept which can become unexpectedly confusing for even experienced report writers, and has become increasingly difficult as a result of report software which will automatically number each paragraph of a report. I am not a fan of this software as it tends to make writers reluctant to make paragraph breaks (a whole new set of numbers seems so much more of a commitment than just pressing the return key) and it can result in writers forgetting that they, rather than the machine, are in control of the material and the way it is arranged. Of course, you may be in a situation where you have to use this software, for example if you are working from an organisation's template; if this is not the case, you might want to stick instead to the traditional rule of reports: that each heading has a number but that paragraphs remain unnumbered. Whichever way you work things, what would still not be expected in a report would be heading without numbers.

Decimal notation is a way to indicate to the reader the level of heading you are offering. This shows not just the level of importance you ascribe to a certain section of information or argument, but also how that section fits into a larger section and the report as a whole.

So, for example, a report entitled 'The impact of a coalition government on social mobility' might have this basic structure:

The Impact of a Coalition Government on Social Mobility

1.0 Introduction

2.0 Coalition governments and business

3.0 Coalition governments: the political impact

4.0 Financial stability under coalition governments

5.0 The societal response to being governed by a coalition

6.0 Conclusions

You would then want to demonstrate that your material is divided further:

The Impact of a Coalition Government on Social Mobility

1.0 Introduction

1.1 Background

1.2 Scope

1.3 Recent coalition governments

2.0 Coalition governments and business

2.1 Business and coalitions

2.2 The European situation

3.0 Coalition governments: the political impact

3.1 Wartime coalitions

3.2 Peacetime coalitions

4.0 Financial stability under coalition governments

4.1 The need for coalitions

4.2 The challenge for coalitions

4.3 The short-term impact of a coalition

4.4 The long-term impact of a coalition

5.0 The societal response to being governed by a coalition

5.1 Social disharmony

5.2 Social stability

5.3 Social mobility

6.0 Conclusions

... and, perhaps, further still:

The Impact of a Coalition Government on Social Mobility

1.0 Introduction

1.1 Background

1.2 Scope

1.3 Recent coalition governments

(Continued)

This use of decimal notation shows the reader instantly (through the table of contents) not only what material is being included in the report, but also how your argument is likely to develop. Naturally, the reader will tend to follow your lead and weigh evidence and its importance to the argument based upon the decimal notation hierarchy you have imposed upon it.

Top Tip

Whilst there are some professional documents, such as specifications, which can routinely become very complicated, for most reports three levels of heading are sufficient (for example, 1.2.4 as your lowest level of heading). There is, of course, no reason why you should not go lower than this, but if you find that you are planning to a fifth or sixth level of heading you might want to check whether this is really what you need, or whether perhaps you have not included enough main headings.

Decimal notation can seem simple enough. Once you are in the midst of actually writing a report, things can become much less obvious. As you type you could sometimes find yourself wondering if you are working under a level two or level three heading, especially if the heading was several pages ago. If you had not planned thoroughly this would be the point where you would have to start scrabbling back through your notes to work out where you are. A plan captures your information and harnesses your argument, but it also keeps you on track with decimal notation and can be a real boon as you write.

Top Tip

I always find it useful to work out the heading numbers for a report at the planning stage. This saves me from the uncomfortable feeling as I write the report of trying to recall under which level of heading I am currently writing, and where I was planning to go next. It also reassures me that, although I am working through material that I have already mentioned in an earlier section, I had always planned to do this so as to examine it from several angles during the course of the report.

The final diagram above, showing the report numbering for my plan, assumes that the writer has the entire structure of the document and the flow of the argument already worked out and ready to go. In reality, you might produce a plan so as to decide how to group the information, and then have to take a further step by considering how your document should best be structured. You might do this just by staring at the spider chart and visualising how the argument would work best. If it does not come clear, you could try using a clock chart. This is not one of my four main methods of planning, but it can be a useful subsidiary tool in what you are trying to do.

The clock chart will rely on you having already produced a spider chart with which you are happy. For the sake of this example it might perhaps be relatively simple:

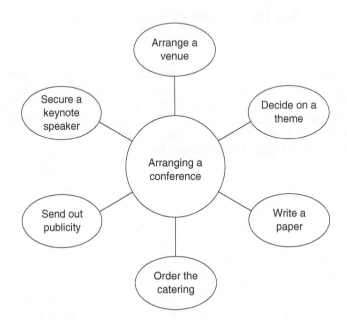

You would then draw a clock face on a piece of paper and place each of the main points from your spider chart in position, as you expect to see them in your dissertation or report. Most writers prefer not to start at midnight, feeling that this might inhibit them from changing their minds and putting a point before that on the chart. After some thoughts, and probably some false starts, the clock chart for this material could look like the figure on the facing page.

You will notice that I have included the hand of the clock at the first point to be covered. This might seem unnecessarily literal, but writers who use clock charts often find this a useful reminder that they have been drawing a clock. These are the writers who find it difficult to motivate themselves to keep writing once they have begun a document. They start with great gusto and then seem to lose heart. For these writers, putting the clock hand on the chart spurs them on. When they are writing up the material around the one o'clock point on the chart they can glance down if they start to lose motivation and remind themselves that they only have, say, two hours of the clock face left to cover.

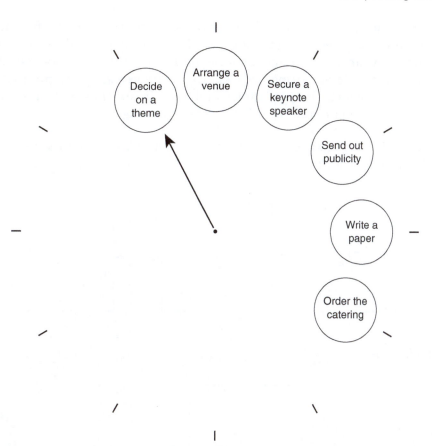

You might find it useful to produce the outline of a blank clock face on a piece of paper and then photocopy or print it out several times. This seems to make it easier for writers to change their minds. If the order in which you are inserting material onto the clock face starts to look awry to you, you can just throw the chart away and begin on a fresh one straight away.

The flowchart

A flowchart will not necessarily throw up lots of ideas that you wouldn't have considered in a spider chart, so the material for each would probably look similar if you were to produce them for the same topic, but it is a fundamentally different process in organising your material. It is a tightly structured way to view your material and, as a result of this, it can encourage in you a more succinct style of writing, with shorter sentences and paragraphs and a greater use of charts, graphs, tables and lists. It can thus be helpful if you know that you tend to ramble a little in your writing.

1. A flow chart begins with a series of boxes; these can work across or down the page. So, they might look like this:

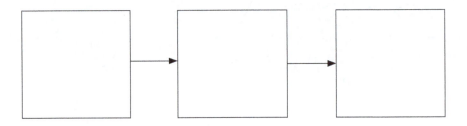

... or like this:

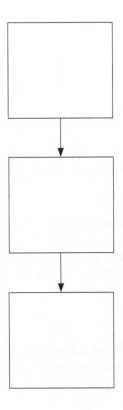

2. You fill in the boxes with your material. Although you may end up producing several versions of a spider chart as your ideas about an argument develop, the flowchart plan is designed to encourage you to order your thoughts as you go. A basic flowchart might be relatively straightforward:

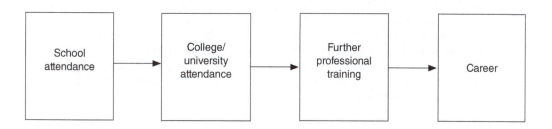

3. The writer might then complicate the flowchart by inserting subsidiary points until it looks more like this:

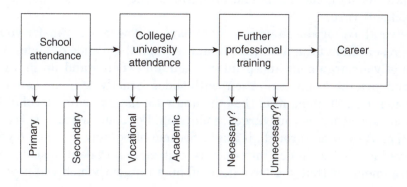

As you will already have gathered, flowcharts work especially well if you are trying to describe a process, or give a set of instructions, or simply convey information in a logical way. It should be possible to see at a glance if you have missed a component out of the sequence; it is for this reason that writers often find flowcharts satisfying and reassuring. They can also be a useful tool in meetings if you want everyone to grasp from one sheet of paper the process you are trying to describe.

Top Tip

There is one danger with any method of planning: it really has to work for the way you think. Some writers find spider charts a little messy and confusing, but others find a flowchart impossible to produce with confidence. I, for example, can rarely see if I have missed anything out and I am resistant to changing the order of the boxes because it always looks perfect to me the first time I produce it. As a result of this, I avoid flowcharts because, for me, they are not a safe planning method. If you are not sure if they would work for you, try offering a flowchart you have produced to some 'critical friends' and ask whether they can spot any gaps.

With either the spider chart or the flowchart method you may still struggle with one aspect of your organisation: how can you be fairly sure that you are reaching your readership? That you are not boring the readers? Or writing at too high or low a level for their understanding? That what you include is relevant and that your argument remains engaging throughout the report or dissertation? Much of the advice in this guide is aiming to help you avoid these pitfalls, but there is a subsidiary planning method which some writers find helpful if they know that they struggle to remain focused on the needs and interests of their readers. They use presentation software.

Once you have produced your spider chart or flowchart, transfer your plan into a presentation format on your computer, making a slide or slides for each section of your argument and printing them off. Then stand up in an empty room and give the full presentation, with slides, exactly as if you had an audience watching you, imagining that the audience has the same level of knowledge and experience as your target readership. For some writers, this can be a revelation. As you go through, it might become blindingly obvious to you that you have included too much introductory material and taken too long to reach your argument, or that you have gone off on a tangent which you now realise is irrelevant.

As you give the presentation, mark on your hard-copy slides with a large marker pen. Cross through the sections where you now feel your document would be too densely packed with largely irrelevant information; put a question mark beside any section which you feel needs to be reassessed; put a plus sign by any section which clearly requires more background information or explanation. You will end up with a series of presentations slides which you have pulled apart and with a far greater sense of how your document should be structured so as to reach your reader.

The brainstorm

Brainstorming is not a complete planning method in itself; rather it is a means to an end, a way to bring up ideas and throw open possibilities before you then begin to order them.

1. The first stage of a brainstorm can look just like a spider chart:

2. The next stage involves putting a series of ideas around this central point. You will be thinking as widely as possible, so odd thoughts, stray ideas and tangential theories would all be included.

This second stage is often undertaken by a group; brainstorms are perhaps best known as effective techniques for team building or generating group ideas. The writer (or perhaps one of the co-writers) might pass the pen around the table so as to give everyone a chance to contribute, or might be standing at the front of the room with a flipchart or smartboard, jotting down the ideas as they arise. There is no great sense of responsibility with a brainstorm because there are no connecting lines. Nobody at this stage is trying to say how a point might be useful, or where it might be incorporated into an argument: they are just ideas and useful bits of information.

Top Tip

The reason why brainstorms work so well as team-building exercises is that everyone feels obliged and able to add to the brainstorm. If you are leading a group brainstorm, make sure that everyone does feel obliged to contribute (you can ask each member in turn to add an idea) and avoid the temptation to pass comment on anyone's idea. If you have shy members of the team, or more junior members who might hesitate to put forward an idea, a brainstorm is a good way to draw them in as long as they are made to feel safe and valued as team members.

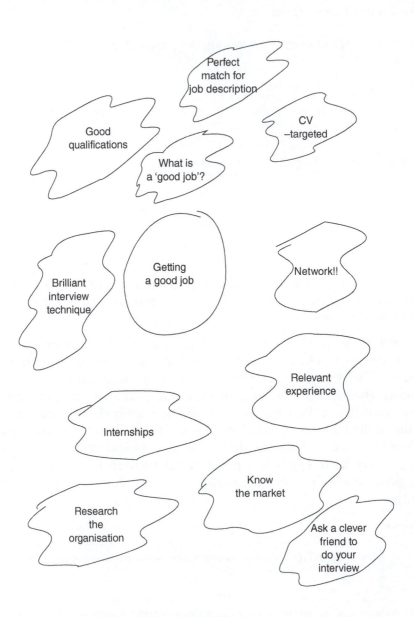

3. Although brainstorms are designed to generate ideas, they also need to be controlled at some stage. If you are the person holding the pen, warn the group in advance that you are not able to guarantee that every single point will make it into the final document. Once the brainstorm session is over, you need to make a judgement on what will be included, what might possibly be included, and what will be discarded at this early stage. Try not to be too polite about anyone's idea: you need to control the information if you are to create a persuasive argument. Of course, if you are producing the brainstorm yourself this moment is much easier.

This stage can look a little destructive:

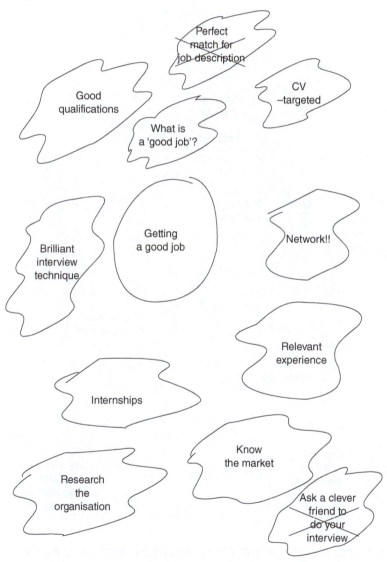

4. Once you have decided what will be kept for the next stage of planning, you might want to look again at the brainstorm. It is at this point that a brilliant way to open your dissertation or report might strike you from the ideas which have emerged: brainstorms often seem to encourage this type of creative thinking, and opening your dissertation or report with an original and intriguing thought is a powerful way to engage your reader. Mark this idea out as one to keep for this purpose:

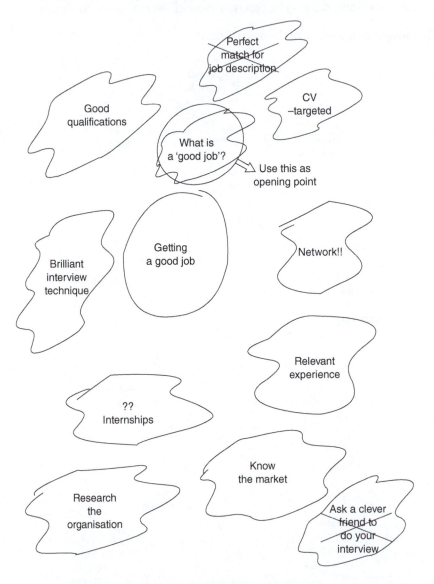

5. Remember that an online brainstorm can be as useful as this pen and paper method, so from here you might want to move to an online brainstorm if your initial paper brainstorm has not produced enough material, either in quantity or variety.

There are three circumstances in which brainstorms tend to be especially valuable: if you are working in a team, if you feel that you have missed a point in your argument, and if you want to find a striking opening for a document. A brainstorm which you produce alone need not take more than a few minutes on a scrap of paper, and it can help to get you thinking creatively before you submit your thoughts to more a structured planning method.

Top Tip

You may have noticed throughout this chapter that I have referred to pen and paper, rather than keyboard and computer screen. This is largely a personal preference, although it is supported anecdotally by many writers with whom I have worked. By producing plans on a piece of paper with a pen, I find that I recall each section better than I would do from a typewritten document; my plan is unique to me, somehow more human and more accessible. I also avoid the common pitfall of producing a computer-generated plan that covers sixteen sheets of A4 and is almost unmanageable. This does not mean, however, that a plan needs to lack detail: an overview spider chart might be accompanied by a series of additional spider charts, each one representing one section of the document.

The mind map

A mind map is a creative document which is, as a result, not easy to pin down and describe: each mind map is unique to its creator. A search online of images of mind maps would give you a good idea of how they end up; here I will offer some guidelines that I have found useful:

1. A mind map begins in the centre of the page. This might be words in a circle, like a spider chart:

Making
perfect
coffee

… because this is a mind map you are likely also to find an image in this space:

… or perhaps you will decide that there is no need for words at all:

… equally, you might favour an image with no enclosing circle:

2. Already you can see that there is plenty of scope in how you produce your mind map, and now you need to add colour. Generally, you would use at least three colours at each 'station' on a mind map; that is, at every place where you are going to stop and look at a point which will become the next stage of your document:

Although we tend to remember best if we see a section which uses at least three colours, one could argue that this is not being used as a memory tool in this context. You are not producing a mind map as a way to revise ready for an exam, but you are producing a document at which you can glance and know exactly where you are going next.

It is for this reason that mind maps can work well if dyslexia is affecting your ability to organise material effectively. They do not need to contain any words at all if this suits you best and, once done, they make sense as complete entities and do not invite constant reworking of the material.

Top Tip

Mind maps also work well if you are not a natural planner, overcoming your tendency to ignore any plan that you make until late in the writing process. This can lead to a strange 'bunching' of material at points in a document when a writer has clearly just remembered to look at the plan and is now trying to catch up with whatever was originally intended. Mind maps linger in the brain and so can help to avoid this problem and smooth out your document.

3. There need be no straight lines on a mind map, nor should you need to turn your head to read sections which are going around the side of the page. You should be able to read the mind map across from left to right with no problem:

4. Some writers find 'spare lines' unhelpful in a mind map and so would ensure that every line is entirely covered by the text it supports:

… others will not want any lines at all and will just use symbols or images to connect their thoughts into a structure from which they can write:

… some will have very few connections, using the space more loosely to define how they would like their argument to develop:

Mind maps do not seem to have much effect on your writing style, but they do seem to have an impact on the confidence of writers. The fact that you are unlikely to change your mind once you have completed a mind map can offer a positive sense of security as you write. Also, if you are not entirely sure of your views on an issue, a mind map can help you to disrupt all of the material and reconfigure it in a way which helps you to work out how your central argument should develop.

Some writers become so keen on mind maps that they use them not only to plan their writing but also to record it after the event. Once a document is complete they will return to their mind map and add any points which they included as they wrote but had not initially intended to use. In this way every aspect of the document is incorporated into the final mind map, which is then filed away for future reference. If ever that writer is asked to work on a similar project in the future, getting back up to speed will be simple and speedy.

Top Tip

Some writers find mind maps especially useful for long-term projects and for team projects. A mind map is begun as soon as the project commences and every time a new aspect of the project opens up the mind map is amended to include this activity and its impact upon the project as a whole. In this way nothing is lost and, if it is a team project, the mind map can be a large laminate sheet on the wall, to which each member of the team can add from time to time.

I have already suggested that some writers find spider charts a little messy and distracting and that other writers find flowcharts too rigid. One of the odd aspects of mind maps, in my experience, is that those who seem to laugh at the very idea of producing a mind map are often the very same writers who, once they try it, come to love this method and will not be persuaded to use anything else. With this in mind, give it a try. I am not a prolific creator of mind maps as planning tools but I do find them useful for recording events at meetings: they are far quicker to produce than it takes to write up notes as people are talking.

Where next?

Once you have worked through one of the planning methods described here, or your own method which you have developed, you might be tempted to plunge straight into writing. I would advise against this, for most writers. There are those who can happily produce a lengthy dissertation or multi-layered report from a spider chart; there are far more who think that they can do this but actually produce rather muddled documents as a result.

If you want to make things easy on yourself, I would suggest instead that you take a different approach. First, go back to the six-point plan with which you started this journey. In the light of what is written on that list of points, is there anything you would like to change in your more detailed plan? Is there an area you have overlooked completely and which you now need to include? Or perhaps you had expected to cover an area which you are now happy to have abandoned. This brief interrogation of your initial ideas will confirm for you that you are in the right place to move ahead.

Once you are content with the choices you have made, it is usually best to transfer your detailed plan into a list of headings and subheadings, even if you will not be including headings in your final document (this is often referred to as a 'list plan'). So, you will take your spider chart (or clock chart, if you went this far) or your flowchart, presentation slides or mind map and transfer each heading onto a separate sheet of paper, following each with a series of subheadings, if you have these, and, if you like, a few bullet points of material you would want to include under each heading or subheading.

Although I have confidently suggested here that you might want to make the odd bullet point beneath a heading or subheading before you happily move on to writing, for many writers this is not an easy transition. Even a detailed plan can seem a long way from a written document. If you feel like this about the task ahead of you, and the gap between planning and writing is beginning to feel more like a chasm, there is no need to panic. Instead, keep adding to these bullet points. Note down the material you want to include in each section; you might even, perhaps, be able to include the odd sentence or two which you think would work well. In this way you can effectively dupe yourself. If you refuse to give up and just keep adding to the list plan you will reach a tipping point where you feel that the thing is almost written already, so clear will your idea of the document be. That is the point where your anxiety will subside and you can seamlessly move from planning to writing.

If you are relatively new to the task of producing lengthy documents which need planning, you might have thought of the planning process as no more than a way to arrange data in your document before you write. I hope, by now, that you can see that it is so much more than this. It is a way of clarifying your views, of structuring your supporting material and of testing the strength of your argument. It also gives you space and time to think about your readers and how you can best persuade them to share your views. You need to do all of this before you take the plunge down the ski slope which is writing.

PART FOUR

Pausing

In the last few paragraphs of the previous chapter I was considering with you how to bridge the gap between planning and writing, especially if the pause between the two became too long. Now I am returning to pauses, negative, necessary and positive. This part, like many of your writing pauses, will be relatively brief but it will be necessary if you are to produce at your best. We will get the negative pauses out of the way first ...

15

Negative pauses

Planning too far

Although I have suggested that you keep working on your list plan, adding material and maybe writing the odd sentence or two, try to ensure that this is a productive activity rather than simply a way to avoid actually writing the document. If the pauses between writing anything on the list plan move from natural moments for thought to protracted breaks away from it, it is time to recognise that you are stalling. Either leave it alone entirely for a day or two in the hope that you will return to it, be inspired by what you have done so far and want to write, or consider whether you might have writer's block and take steps to solve this common writing problem.

Writer's block

Writer's block is not always as one might see it on the television: an anguished writer sitting at a desk, utterly without inspiration and unable to write anything at all. Sometimes it is more a case of hesitating for too long before each new writing session, or pausing for an unnecessarily long time between sections, paragraphs and sentences. These pauses may be almost imperceptible to start with, but after some little while you will begin to notice them more and more, by which time they will be draining your confidence and making you question yourself at every point in your writing.

  Although writer's block can be crippling for some writers at some points in their writing life, for most of us, for most of the time, it is no more than a nuisance. We take a break away from writing and return later, or the next day, to find that all is well again.

Top Tip

Sometimes what we perceive to be writer's block is, in fact, no more than a natural state of tiredness after the exertion of writing for an extended period without a break. Before you rush to assume that you have a problem with writer's block, take a break and return, refreshed, to your writing. Only if the difficulty persists should you consider some of the solutions offered here.

I have listed below some of the most common causes of writer's block, both that which causes an occasionally and/or repeated difficulty and that which seizes up your writing altogether.

Boredom → you may have been working too intensely for too long or, funnily enough, you might be feeling isolated, even if there are people working all around you. Take a break (not too long – time yourself to take only fifteen minutes or so) and talk to colleagues or friends. If your writing speeds up significantly when you return to it, you will know that you just need to take more regular breaks.

Distraction → it takes training to resist distractions, or to deal with necessary distractions and get back to writing without any great loss of concentration. If you know that you are unable to avoid some distractions, and that you are not very good at returning to your writing effectively, try taking the next section of your plan and breaking it down into even more detail that you already have. Bullet point not just headings or sections, but also paragraphs. That way, if you are interrupted you are less likely to waste time trying to find your way back into your writing.

Top Tip

Only produce a plan as detailed as this if you know that you have a problem with distractions and you are sure that you can work well with such an exhaustive plan. For some writers, such a thorough plan would actually make it more difficult for them to write, thus in itself proving to be a distraction.

Information overload → your planning will have helped you to sort the material which is relevant to your argument from the material which you can discard, but this could still leave you with a huge amount of information to include in your dissertation or report. It might also be the case that you have done so much reading and research that you are feeling pressure to include too much material so as to justify all of the work you have undertaken. If this is making you anxious and reluctant to write anything, produce an overview list plan (that is, a plan which looks like a table of contents but with only the main sections listed) so that you can take a step back and remind yourself of your ultimate goal. You could also try producing the clock chart I described in the previous section of this guide: it can be an excellent motivator.

Too much responsibility → if you have planned well you should, at least in theory, be ready to write with confidence, but this is not always the case if you are suddenly struck by the importance of what you are trying to do. Nerves set in, you increase the pressure on yourself by remembering how important this is to you, your anxiety levels rise and you start to seize up mentally. If this feels familiar go back to your plan. Do you have confidence in it? Is there one aspect of it about which you have concerns? Have you discussed it in detail with your mentor, supervisor or boss? If you can assure yourself that your plan is sound, it is safe to assume that you just need a structured break. Give yourself and hour or so and do something completely unrelated to your document: you should return with a renewed determination.

Too much work → worrying about other tasks to be completed or leaving yourself inadequate time to write up a document can cause significant problems for writers. Rather than speeding up the writing process, as you might logically expect, this type of pressure usually slows down your ability to write and might even stop you being able to write altogether. It is rarely possible to jettison all of your other tasks in favour of writing one document, but it is often relatively easy to prioritise your tasks, once you come to address this problem. You might find that producing a timetable to show your expected completion date and how you aim to get there could help. It can also be useful to set aside a time each day to write, either a specific time of day, during which you are unlikely to be distracted by other work, or plan to type for, say, two hours each day.

Top Tip

Some writers prefer to allocate a number of words that they plan to produce each day rather than setting aside a time to write. Having a word target can work well for some, less well for others, so experiment with this technique if you feel it might help but be prepared to move away from it if the writing challenge is not becoming easier. If you are going to produce a target number of words per day, make sure that the target is realistic and helpful: 200 words a day, for example, might lead to a disjointed style of writing.

Loss of confidence → this could be confidence in your document or in your ability to produce it. Either way, it can be damaging to your writing fluency and your work rate. Completing just one task, either within your writing (getting to the end of a section, or producing a diagram or other insert) or away from it (filing away some research material, answering an email which has been bothering you) can have a surprisingly beneficial effect on your confidence.

Top Tip

If your loss of confidence persists, it can manifest itself not in a hesitancy in writing but in an unproductive way of writing. You question yourself to the point where you rewrite sentences several times, trying to perfect them, or delete and reorganise whole paragraphs or sections of your work. This can be incredibly time consuming and tiring and is, of course, largely unproductive if taken to the point where it is getting in the way of your overall productivity. In this situation it can help to share your ideas and your plans for the work with a supportive colleague or friend. If this is a recurring problem for you both, you could arrange regular times to meet up and inspire each other.

Struggling to focus → if this is not usually a problem for you then it could have a physical cause. Try not to be writing at the time of day when you usually find your energy levels dipping and, of course, make sure that you are getting enough sleep if this is possible. Eat high energy foods if this will help you to keep going. Dehydration is a major contributor to lack of focus so ensure that you have water to hand. If you begin to suspect that the cause is not physical, make sure that you are writing for what you know is the optimum exertion time for you. If you write for very much longer than usual it is only natural that you will find yourself struggling to keep alert.

Loss of words → this is a strange form of writer's block in that it does not make you pause in your writing; instead it leaves you reaching vainly for the right word, or using words and phrases which you know are not quite right for the context and your meaning, or overusing a word because you simply cannot think of a better word to express a meaning. This problem will right itself in time, but in the meantime you need to develop the use of your own personal marker system. This allows you the opportunity to mark up your work as you go, noting where there are problems. Some writers inset a few XXXs before what they think might be the wrong use of a word, some use the highlighter function to note sentences which do not quite work, some change the font colour in those paragraphs where they are not sure that they are making the strongest possible argument. I press the hash key three times (###) to show that I need to return to that point in the text later to consider whether it works well.

Top Tip

When you first start to use a personal marker system it can actually make you feel less confident in your writing for a few days. It is as if, because you can question yourself, you do question yourself. This will ease quickly and you will find the system useful, but be ready to see pages scattered with personal markers whenever you become tired or anxious.

What I have offered you here is a suite of solutions to one recurring problem. If you can identify the cause of your writer's block, you are far more likely to be able to find a timely solution. However it manifests itself in your writing, and however frustrating you find it, you can gain comfort from the fact that it is most unlikely to be a long-term problem.

Dyslexia

If you are already aware of your needs around dyslexia, you probably already have strategies in place to help you maximise your efficiency despite this challenge. If you suspect you might have dyslexia, you need to seek an accurate diagnosis, whether you are a student or a professional. The vague feeling that you might be dyslexic, which can sometimes be based on little more than an article you have read, or a comment someone made about your writing, can be debilitating, making you unnecessarily anxious about your ability to write.

You might have to incur the cost of obtaining a diagnosis, but this is not always the case: many organisations will fund this for their students or staff. It is only once you have been diagnosed that you will get a sense of where you sit on the dyslexia spectrum; this will be important in helping you gain expert advice on a strategy. The good news is that, in many cases, the solution can be easy to implement and no great distraction to how you work already.

Colleges, universities and commercial organisations frequently have extensive support systems in place to help, but this is not always well advertised. In addition, some writers are reluctant to seek help, afraid that they will be labelled in some way, or suffer discrimination as a result. If they have failed to mention their dyslexia on an application form they are even more anxious about the situation. Although there is no way to guarantee that every single person you meet will understand dyslexia and be supportive of your efforts to overcome this challenge, in my experience I have found overwhelmingly that dyslexia is met with a positive and practical approach from academic and commercial organisations and the staff who work within them.

Interruptions and procrastination

We tend to think of an interruption as something which is done to us and we are far less aware of how often we interrupt ourselves; this section will deal with both. Being interrupted is, for most of us, a regular part of our daily lives. If we are trying to work in a busy environment we will obviously suffer more interruptions and, of course, for many people the interruption of a phone call or a colleague asking for help is part of their workload.

Trying to reduce the number of interruptions at all times can be more stressful than just putting up with them, and the grumpy writer in the corner is probably not a persona that you would want to assume. It is usually easier to set up a system whereby you can banish interruptions altogether for some part of the day. If you know that interruptions ruin your concentration, and you are working in a commercial environment, consider setting up a swap system whereby a colleague will take calls and answer queries on your behalf for, say, a couple of hours twice a week in exchange for you repaying the favour on other days. If you use this time to focus on nothing but writing, you will be delighted at how much you can achieve, and how much you can produce in those two hours will rise with each passing week.

Top Tip

Be careful to avoid becoming too fond of interruptions. They can be hugely seductive, giving us a legitimate reason to leave our work for a short while and allowing us to talk to colleagues and friends. They can also make us feel important: clearly people are relying on us if we cannot spend even an hour writing without someone needing our help. This is a dangerous position for a writer, so beware of allowing yourself to fall into it.

If you cannot negotiate a swap system you might instead consider going into work or your place of study early so as to avoid the crowds, or arranging to work from home once a week so that you can write uninterrupted. If neither of these is possible, you will have to develop a way to minimise the disruptive influence of interruptions. The easiest way I have found to do this is to use the personal marker system I described earlier. Whenever anyone appears or your phone rings, insert your personal marker (XXX or ### or whatever) and deal with the interruption. Handle it as speedily as you can and then look back to the screen. You will have the option of deleting your marker and resuming where you were, or, if you feel you have lost your way, you can abandon that point for now and move on to the next point in your plan. Later, you can go back to the marker and focus on finishing the section or sections which had been left due to interruptions.

This technique also works well for those times when you interrupt yourself, but first you have to identify whether this is an issue for you as a writer. There are several ways in which we tend to interrupt ourselves:

- Pausing to try to think of the right word.
- Rereading a sentence because it did not seem quite right as we wrote it.
- Rewriting that sentence – sometimes several times.

- Rereading a paragraph or even a whole section, wondering if it is as persuasive and authoritative as we would like it to be.
- Rewriting that section, or parts of it.
- Reworking our plan, because we are not sure if it is good enough, even though the writing stage has begun.
- Quickly nipping onto our email/social network system to see if we have a reply to a message we sent earlier.
- Making a list of all the things we will be able to get done later in the day, once the writing is over.
- Looking out of the window and daydreaming, almost without realising we are doing it.
- Beginning a text conversation just before we start to write, a conversation which we know will provide regular, brief interruptions for hours.
- Deciding that we have not done enough preparation, abandoning writing altogether for the day and reverting to the safety of the plan, reworking it yet again.
- Feeling so uninspired that we go to an online chat room related to our area of work, so that we can talk to others who are also supposed to be writing in a similar area, but who are also interrupting themselves.

I wrote in the previous paragraph that this might be 'an issue' for you, rather than assuming it need be a problem. For some of us, these minor interruptions (some just a few seconds long) are a natural part of the rhythm of our writing and so are productive, giving us a moment to regain our bearings and think out our next point. Only if they become so frequent or lengthy that they risk interrupting the flow of your writing and thinking too much will you need to conquer the habit.

If you work through the list above, considering whether you have fallen into the habit of pausing in any of these ways, you will already be on the road to fixing the problem. This is one of those times when just becoming conscious of a problem helps you to avoid it. If this is not enough, use the personal marker system to force yourself to keep moving despite your tendency to interrupt yourself. If you persevere with this over a few weeks you will find that you come to interrupt yourself less and your writing process will flow far better.

Although I have been exploring here the issue of interruptions, the later items on this list need not necessarily be happening whilst you are actually writing: they may prevent you from beginning writing altogether. In this way, interruptions turn into procrastination: a different term but the effect is the same. Procrastination is usually easier to spot that self-made interruptions. If you are happily chatting away online when you had planned to write, there will be a niggling voice in the back of your mind telling you that you really should be writing. If this is not a frequent problem for you, ignore it; we all need a break some time. However, if you find that time is slipping by and you are not producing much writing, you need to take action.

Work out why you are putting off the moment of writing and forgive yourself the delay; feeling guilty about not getting on with it is not going to help you. I will outline here six key reasons for procrastination. Luckily, the fix is usually relatively simple:

1. You have never noticed that you tend to procrastinate, but you knew that you were a bit slow to produce anything → this section will have made you aware of this and that in itself will help.
2. You do not feel like writing today, but you know that you should → there is often a physical cause for this. If you feel tired, hungry, thirsty or unwell, you will probably be better off rescheduling the writing session until you are physically in a better position, refusing to allow yourself to feel bad about it.
3. You want to write, but you just cannot seem to get on with it → check the section earlier in this chapter on writer's block.
4. You worked hard in your last writing session and did not seem to produce much, which has put you off → check again to see whether you are interrupting yourself as you write.
5. You are unsure where you are going, so there seems little point in writing → this can lead to both procrastination and interruptions, so go back to your plan *before* you begin your writing session and take the next section on which you were planning to write. Ignore the rest for now and just work on that section of the plan, modifying it if you need to. Then write that section up and only go back to your overall plan once that has been achieved.
6. You dread every writing session, feeling sure that you will not be able to produce much or that your writing quality will be poor. You are starting to wonder why you ever thought you could write a whole dissertation or report and you are sick to death of trying → an experienced writer will know that sometimes this feeling can be followed by an amazingly good writing session, but if you are feeling this despondent about what you are doing then it is safest to take a constructive break. Rather than ignoring the problem, talk to someone. A mentor, colleague, friend or supervisor will be able to help, not necessarily by working through the detail of your work with you, but perhaps simply by sharing the problem, confessing that they sometimes feel the same and reminding you that they have confidence in you.

As you can see from the litany of pauses in this chapter, there are many ways in which you can allow others to ruin your flow of writing; there are also myriad ways in which you can sabotage yourself. However, pauses are not always a bad thing. Indeed, there are many necessary pauses in the production of a document, and it is to these that we will turn now.

16

Necessary pauses

The analogy I have used throughout this guide, of writing being akin to a downhill ski slope, includes the suggestion that you will sometimes need to stop for a short while so as to get your bearings. It is on that part of the ski run that I want to concentrate now, so that you can recognise, and make the most of, the pauses which are a necessary part of writing a dissertation or report.

Finding the time to write

You will face a potential barrage of interruptions and distractions if you write at a time and in a place which is not conducive to a peaceful writing session. Added to this, you also need to consider the best time of day for you to write. Of course you will need to accept that life is not perfect, and that you will not always be able to write at your preferred time of day, but we tend to listen to myths about this ('everyone works at their best in the morning', 'there is no point in trying to write after sunset', 'always write before a meal rather than after' and so forth) and this can hinder you finding the best writing time for you.

It might be that you have never given this any thought before – most of us have not considered it until someone points out to us how important it is. Try to avoid assumptions that you have (or have been told) about yourself: being a 'night owl' or a 'morning lark' might be a response to a work schedule or a partner's lifestyle rather than your true preferred time to work. Even if you do tend to feel cheerful and upbeat in the morning, this still might not mean that it is the best writing time for you. Rather than assuming, take a more scientific approach and time your output (as I suggested in the earlier chapter 'Gathering material') to see how well you are working after, say, an hour in the morning and compare this to how well you perform after an hour in the evening.

Top Tip

We usually have a time of day during which we work at our optimum rate, but for some writers the variation in output at different times of the day is negligible. If this is the case for you, you will be in the lucky position of being able to work your writing schedule around your other commitments without any loss of efficiency.

Finding your confidence

Much of this guide so far has been about you working through a process in order to get to the point where you can write in a way which is productive and will achieve your desired end. I was writing of procrastination and interruptions in the last chapter, and earlier on in the book we considered together the challenges of losing confidence and how to keep going despite any obstacles. All of this might, understandably, have left you with the impression that all pauses are problematic. In fact, we all tend to prefer taking a little time before we write, readying ourselves for the task ahead.

This pause is small, but it is necessary. It does not involve actually doing anything, but, having made the plan and committed yourself to writing, a short pause allows you to garner confidence in what you are about to do. Having scheduled the writing of this guide, for example, I spent a few days waiting for the moment when I was going to write. I did not add to the plan, I did not change my mind about my goals and I did not begin on any draft chapters. I just took time to let my brain idly contemplate what was going to happen. It is a trick that many writers use, so do not be afraid to allow this constructive pause to happen.

Taking time to reflect

Being able to pause as you write, just momentarily and from time to time, is a natural and necessary part of the creative process. It is not the same as procrastination, which is done with no reference to the point you have reached in your writing and does not work into the natural rhythm of that process.

You may not think that you have a rhythm to your writing, but you do – we all do. I know, for example, that I tend to pause after about six sentences to have a glance back at where I have been and where I am going. Creating a rhythm seems to be part of human endeavour in all sorts of activities. Watch someone knitting and you will see that they lay the garment out in front of them to check it every now and then. In a gym you will see exercisers who put a towel over the dashboard on the exercise machine they are using, only checking their calorie burn at intervals.

This rhythm in your writing is related to the person you are (those who fidget tend to glance back on their writing more often, for example) and on how you are feeling (a writer confident in what is being written might look back less frequently). Now that you know you will be doing this, and that it can be a positive part of your writing experience, you can work to increase its impact:

- Notice each day's rhythm → if you are pausing to reflect much more frequently than normal, see this as a sign that something is not comfortable for you and take steps, if you can, to fix it. This might be a physical fix (have you drunk enough water today?) or a mental fix (are you clear about what you are trying to say in this section of your report or dissertation?).
- Time yourself → pauses for reflection usually take less than a minute. In that time you will be able to look back and read a few paragraphs, perhaps a few pages, but no more than that. You will then resume writing, hardly aware that you had stopped. If the pause is longer, it need not be a problem as you will be giving your mind a rest as well as reviewing your activity. This longer break will not, for most people, be more than 5–10 minutes.
- Make it a positive pause → have a constructive activity, linked to your project, to fill the pauses each time they happen, and try to do something similar each time you pause. This might be reading the last section of your work out loud to make sure that your writing voice is not changing its tone, or visualising your supposed readers for a moment, imagining that you are talking to them rather than writing alone.
- Keep to a routine → for longer pauses (of, say, 10–20 minutes) try to do the same sorts of things each time you pause. This might be making a hot drink or walking around the block. Ideally, these activities would not become distractions, so checking your emails or a social network site would not be a good idea if you know this would lead you astray.
- Work the pattern → if you notice a pattern emerging in these pauses, take note and try to stick to it if it is helping. If you are writing from home, for example, you might write for a while within minutes of waking up, then break to shower and dress, then break a while later for food, then break again for a tea break an hour later and so forth. There is something about the stability of this type of routine that can feel very supportive.
- Reveal your plan only partially → a useful pause is created if you only print out part of your final list plan (your list plan might be the only part of your plan which you have typed out and so can manipulate in this way). You can work through that small section and then pause before you move on to print out and write from the next small section. This can be a useful technique if you find you are taking longer pauses more often than you think is beneficial.

- Before you begin → you can create another type of positive pause before you begin on each writing session. If you resist making spellcheck corrections during a session, they will be waiting for you to do at the start of the next session. Beginning a session by skimming through it as you make spellcheck decisions can be a good way to reacquaint yourself with a sense of where you are before you commit to writing anything.
- At the end of each session → some writers enjoy taking a pause from writing at the end of each session and they reread what they have written. Others find this a less positive pause, so finding out which works for you early in the writing process would be useful.

These pauses are worth recognising and cultivating in your writing sessions: they can become a valuable part of your creative process for many years.

17

Positive pauses

Positive pauses can be less instinctive than those covered in the previous chapter, but you could make them a part of your writing routine and so increase the impact of your writing. They relate to a higher level of writing style than simply being able to convey information: they are about persuading your reader not just by the strength of your argument, but by the way in which you articulate that argument.

The idea of writing persuasively can seem alien to some writers. Surely, you might say, I am trying to do no more in my dissertation than present the results of my research. Or, if you are producing a report, you might wonder why you have to be persuasive, given that reports are supposed to be objective documents. Actually, neither of these positions is entirely accurate. Yes, you are presenting your research findings in a dissertation, but you are also trying to persuade readers of your intellectual integrity and the rigour of your evidence. Your report is objective in that you are trying to put all of the relevant evidence before the reader, but you are necessarily making subjective decisions about which pieces of information you believe are important, and the order in which you include them, and the way in which you write about them.

So, the myth that you are doing no more than objectively presenting evidence in either a dissertation or a report can be dismissed straight away. In its place comes the realisation that every piece of writing you produce is an opportunity to persuade somebody of something. Once this has been accepted, you can use positive pauses alongside the rest of the advice in this guide to ensure that your word is heard and that your argument succeeds.

Keeping on track

One way in which a document can lose its power is if the writer drifts too far away from the main thrust of the argument, either by including material which is largely irrelevant or by writing in a style which is weak or rambling. You do not need to write in a clipped, note-like style, far from it, but I would recommend that you keep your mind firmly on course as you write. If you lose concentration you will find that you stray from the path you had intended.

Funnily enough, the way you will first notice this is likely to be in your writing style rather than in any sense of the content becoming vague or unnecessary. You will be mildly dissatisfied with how you are writing, and this will build until you feel forced to take your fingers off the keyboard and stop for a moment. If at this point you look back at what you have just written, you will see some unimpressive writing and little sense of structure: this is likely to make you even more unsure about your direction. Instead of looking back, add your personal marker where you have stopped and check back to your plan. Remind yourself of all the impressive points you have made, and still have to make, and then go back to writing, beginning at the next point in your plan. Later you can return to the place where your writing went awry and it will be a simple task to correct the problem at that point.

Persuading your reader

Once you have accepted that you are always seeking to persuade in everything you write, you will want to get to grips with the various tools at your disposal for producing writing that is persuasive:

Use headings to guide readers: Although you will be taking the headings in your dissertation or report from your plan, make a point of checking every now and then that the headings are frequent enough and descriptive enough to show the readers where your argument is heading. This will ensure that your readers are ready for the next stage of your argument before they reach the detail. The frequent but brief headings in this guide are an example of how readers can, I hope, be guided and reassured by them.

Give titles to projects and issues: If you want a project to sound impressive or important, it can help if you give it a title; if you need your readers to take notice of an issue, try giving it a title too. You would not want to alienate your readers by lots of titles which are confusing or difficult to grasp, but rather than repeatedly referring to 'the fourth traffic bridge across the River Dee near a main conurbation', you could more effectively refer to it in this descriptive way once and thereafter use your own title for it: 'the fourth Dee crossing'.

Use bullet points to guide the reader on the page: Bullet points are a good way to reassure readers, but they can also help to persuade them. A bullet point tells readers that they can take as long as they need to consider a point and try to understand it. They can even leave the document for a while if they like; when they come back the next bullet point will be sitting there waiting for them. This in itself is useful, but even more useful from your point of view is the fact that readers, once they spot bullet points on a page, will tend to underplay in their mind whatever comes just before the bullet-pointed list. This means that you can insert information which you would rather nobody dwell on too long just above your bullet points, and then include material just after the list which you would like all of your readers to notice.

Use white space to increase accessibility: Readers always respond positively to white space. It makes your writing more accessible and impressive, it ensures that your points are easier to grasp and that your argument flows better in the mind of the reader. It is difficult to overestimate its importance in writing persuasively. Indeed, in the case of a report we usually recognise that it is a report for three reasons: it has an impressive-looking title page, it is a bound document and it contains plenty of white space. This would include wide margins, plenty of space between sections and enough space around graphs, charts and tables to ensure that they stand out impressively and are easy to read.

Use 'signposting' words: 'Signposting' is a way of helping your reader through a document. It can be employed in many ways: using headings as I suggested above, opening each section of a report or dissertation with a brief outline of what you hope to achieve in that section, including a synopsis or abstract with your document, ensuring that your paragraphing works constructively to help the reader. All of these structural signposting techniques can be joined by detailed signposting in the use of words. Signposting words never add anything to the meaning of a sentence; they indicate to the reader how the sentence is to be read.

There are several key signposting words which will help you to write more persuasively with very little effort. If you start a sentence with 'whilst', 'whereas', 'although' or 'despite', your readers will pay scant attention to whatever you write before the comma which you will inevitably include, and will focus on whatever comes after the comma. ('Whilst I would love to meet you for lunch, I am not able to make it today.' 'Despite our best efforts, we were unable to save the whale.') If you begin a sentence with 'however', your reader will know that you are about to turn from one piece of information or point of view to another. If you use 'therefore' or 'in conclusion', your readers' interest will perk up: this must be nearly the end of the document and the main points they need to grasp are about to come up.

Top Tip

Writers often believe that there are rules about the use of the word 'however', as they vaguely recollect a school teacher or style guide suggesting that it should never be used to start a sentence, or that it should (or, sometimes, should never) have a comma after it. It is worth knowing, however, that there are no such rules. When you use it you need to be aware that many people are uneasy about the word. However, it is such a useful signposting word that I would still advocate its use. However hard people resist it, they will be swayed by its power in a sentence.

- **Avoid 'danger signal' phrases**: Having considered how to persuade readers by your writing, you also need to note one way in which readers can be made instantly suspicious of your writing. If, before you have given enough information or forged a persuasive enough line of argument, you include phrases which pre-empt the judgement of the readers, you risk irritating them, even if your assertion is true. Such phrases include 'it is safe to assume', 'it is obvious', 'it is undeniable'.

Naturally, you will want to be as persuasive in your writing as you can be, but be ready for this to take a little time. You will already be using some of these techniques, without especially noticing it, so you need first to identify how well you are doing before you make a deliberate move to incorporate more of them. Pause now and take a piece of your writing (ideally, 4–5 pages) and, with a highlighter pen, mark up your work every time you come across one of the tools for persuasion listed here. The density of the highlighter will show you which of these tools you are using already; you will then be in an excellent position to increase your use of them whenever you like.

Seeking advice

You might pause from time to time to seek advice or ask for feedback on your work to date and you can ensure that these are positive pauses. Distributing drafts of your work is fairly standard practice in both the academic and the professional world, but you need to make this a positive pause.

Online brainstorming: There are times when you seem to have hit a totally negative pause. You look up from your writing because you cannot decide on the next immediate thing to write and then you realise that, in fact, the next few paragraphs are not very clear in your mind either. In trying to concentrate and re-grasp the thread of your thoughts, you come to see that you have lost your way. What seemed clear in the planning stage has, upon reflection, become unclear, even doubtful in its validity.

This is not an easy position in which to find yourself, but it is common enough. First, try to employ the suggestions I made in the previous chapter under the section on 'Taking time to reflect'. It might be that this is all you need. If, when you come back to your writing, you still feel that you are missing something, or you have doubts about an assertion you want to make, try an online brainstorm. This will have two beneficial effects: it will allow your supporters to reassure you, or to offer good advice and useful information to help you out, and it will give you the perfect excuse to walk away from that section of writing for a while. Sometimes this pause is sufficient for things to come clear in your mind again.

Top Tip

If doubts about what you are writing come into your mind quite early in a writing session you have planned, and you decide that you need to use an online brainstorm in order to clarify things, you do not have to desert your writing altogether for that day. Instead, use your personal marker where you have moved away from a section and then get on with writing the next section, or chapter, or stage of your plan. That way you will not risk spending the rest of the day feeling frustrated that you have achieved less than you hoped and worrying unnecessarily about the problem you have encountered. By writing instead, you will be able to build your confidence and remain productive.

Distributing drafts: Asking for feedback on your plan, as I suggested earlier, is one thing; inviting comments on your writing is quite another. A plan is malleable and so subject to change without any great problem, but your writing has taken time to craft, it crystallises what you want to say and you have put thought and emotion into it in a way that can make it hard to receive any criticism, however constructive. For this reason it is worth taking a cautious approach. Decide, before you begin to write, how often you are going to ask for a review. Will it be at the end of the first draft or at several prearranged points in your writing journey? Once these times are set, try to stick to them unless something specific is worrying you about a section of the work.

Once you have decided when to ask for feedback you will need to choose the best pool of critical friends. Ideally, this would include at least one person who has no great interest in the content but who is prepared to look at your work from a layperson's point of view, asking the obvious questions and making sure that it hangs together, and at least one expert in the field who can comment on the content. You might want these critical friends to review the entire document once it is complete in draft form, but you might also ask others to review smaller sections of the report or dissertation.

Before you hand over your writing for review, make sure that your supporters know what is being asked of them. Even if you are hoping for a general review of the work as a whole, you might still have niggling areas of doubt about one or two sections of the work. It can be useful to ask them to review the document in its entirety first, before looking at the specific questions that you have listed about particular sections. That way you will not be swaying their judgement and you are more likely to get comprehensive feedback.

Top Tip

Some writers find distributing drafts of their work for comment unhelpful. This might not be because they have any doubts about their work, as you might assume, but rather because they prefer to produce the polished report or dissertation before they show it to anyone so that they only have one review stage rather than several pauses along the way. Indeed, some writers work so hard on detailed plans that they hardly need to review the overall shape of their writing at all.

Alienating yourself from your work

When it comes to checking and polishing your work I will be urging you to take a break before you revisit your document to check it as this allows you to move away from the text and see it in an objective light. In effect, you will be trying to view it as a reader rather than as its writer. You can begin this process as you write. It is rather strange, when you come to think about it, that writing is about the only thing we produce for which we cannot truly see the result. We take a photo and can admire it; we make a cake and eat it; we write ... into nowhere. Unless you can see it as a reader, all you are doing is rereading something which you produced, assuming it is exactly as you intended it to be rather than how it truly is.

The best way to alienate yourself from your text is to read it out loud to yourself. Not muttering it under your breath in a room full of people, but walking around an empty room reading it aloud, putting expression into it, responding to each piece of punctuation and listening to how it sounds. You will be amazed to discover your writing, perhaps for the first time.

Top Tip

A word of warning: the first time you do this can be unnerving. It can be similar to the experience you get when you hear your voice back on an outgoing telephone message system, or see yourself on film. When you read aloud like this you might sound nothing like you had imagined your writing self to be. You might think you sound pompous, or bored, or irritated, or scared. Be ready for this. It will not actually be as bad as you think it is on the first read-through, and you will now be in the best possible position to correct any problems you have found.

I would suggest that you read sections of your work aloud whenever you start to lose sight of your writing self, or can no longer hear your writing voice clearly. When the work is complete, you would also be wise to read the whole thing aloud one last time: it is by far the most efficient way to find mistakes.

Of course, to be able to employ any of the techniques in this chapter you need to have some writing to examine and improve; the next section will help you to focus on the detail of the writing process.

PART FIVE
Producing

For the vast majority of your writing time you will not be giving the process much thought. This is not the result of carelessness; it is simply that you have no need to think about it. As you write there is a running narrative in your head, as you speak to your reader and transfer it into words on the page. Your mental narrative will be in your 'writing voice' rather than your normal speaking voice, but it will still, generally, be effortless. Because we all have the ability to write in this way, often even if we are writing in our second language, I do not propose to work through with you every aspect of the English language and how it can be used. That is another book altogether. Basic writing guides, which explain each detail of how to write, are plentiful, but here I plan something different for our time together.

What I will be doing in this part is refusing to take a blanket approach to all aspects of writing, but rather concentrating on the help that you are most likely to need. Many years of working with individual clients and students, and teaching groups of professional delegates, has allowed me to pinpoint my advice precisely to the most common areas of need. By working through this part you will be alerted to the pitfalls writers encounter on a regular basis and you will be able to avoid the most common writing mistakes.

It is for this reason that I have divided the part into the tools we have at our disposal: words, sentences and so forth. In each of these chapters you can be confident of finding information about the queries you have and you could also encounter some conventions of good writing which you have not yet considered.

18

Words

Why do they matter?

As I have already suggested, for much of the time our words convey our meaning without any great effort on our part. This is not because the choice of words is not important, but because we know, as if by an acquired instinct, exactly the word that we want to use. We therefore give it little conscious thought, but what if we did? Take the sentence above and the use of the word 'acquired'. I could have left it out altogether, but that would have meant that language use is instinctive. As we are born without being able to speak, this would seem to be inaccurate, however innate our capacity for language. I could have said 'natural instinct', but that would be tautological because an instinct is, by definition, taken to be natural. However, I know that although the way we write *feels* instinctive, it is actually a learned skill. So I used the word 'acquired', aiming to convey to you in the most efficacious way that it is not exactly an instinct, but it is an inherent potential and, once we have learnt to write, it quickly comes to feel natural.

Phew! That is a substantial amount of analysis for one word, but it demonstrates two things. The first is that we are all very good at this writing stuff, even if we doubt it at times. The second is that we have a huge amount of choice about how we do it, even if we do not always think about it much. Clearly, if one single, solitary word can make such a difference, it would be worth anyone's while to learn how to use words to best effect.

One last point before we move on. Word choice is about meaning, but it is also about feel. You might already have noticed how my overall choice of words led to two paragraphs which felt slightly different to read. The first paragraph in this chapter comprised words and punctuation which were relatively formal, perhaps even words which you have not often encountered ('tautological', 'innate', 'efficacious' or 'inherent'). We know each other a little by now and so you probably kept on reading even though it was feeling unfamiliar at times. In the second paragraph I swung the other way, with an exclamation at the outset and then some far more informal, conversational words and phrases ('writing stuff', 'single, solitary word'). You would have found this easy to read, a pleasant break perhaps after the previous paragraph, but you might be a little concerned if I wrote a whole book in this way.

Words to use; words to avoid

It is impossible to give you a definitive list of words which you should use and this is a good thing. It cannot be done because each of us has developed our own vocabulary over years of listening and speaking. We have then filed that vocabulary in our mental dictionary into different categories for styles of speaking: casual, formal, polite, angry. Simultaneously, from the age at which we learn to write, we have been developing a tandem vocabulary category: our written English. This will usually be more precise and formal and, in the case of dissertations or reports, it will often be significantly more formal and specialised than the language we would use in chatting to friends. For each of us, it is important to use our own range of vocabulary and use it in a way which is unique to us: that is what makes our writing human, interesting and persuasive.

So, there is no list out there which will show you the perfect set of words you should use. Indeed, your vocabulary is far broader than you might expect, running to many thousands of words, and so the list would be so vast as to be unusable. I can, however, tell you how you can increase the number of useful and appropriate words at your disposal:

1. Each day, take just a few minutes to read a paragraph of somebody else's text which has been written at, or slightly above, your usual writing style. This might be in a textbook or professional journal, or in a good quality newspaper, for example.
2. Once you have read the paragraph stop and go back. Reread it again more slowly, making a positive effort to notice the words that are being used and the way they are employed.
3. Then reread once more to cement them in your mind, this time noticing the effect they have on you. You need do nothing more than this.
4. An hour or so later you might not consciously remember the paragraph in any great detail, but you might be able to recall a couple of words which particularly left an impression on you. However, you will find that, over time, new words will creep into your language.

This simple exercise can lead to a marked improvement in the number of words you use and can also, as I mentioned in the chapter on finding your voice, elevate you writing style.

Identifying the words that you should avoid is more difficult to tackle. A list of banned words would not help much, because the use of words is all about context: there are few words which it would never, under any circumstances, be appropriate to use. As there is no list available, we can work instead on categories of words to avoid:

- **Groups of simple words where one would suffice**: It is difficult to achieve precision in your writing if your 'writing vocabulary' is not wide enough. You may suffer from this even if your spoken vocabulary is very wide. I sometimes find that students who have been articulate in seminars turn out to be rather stunted in their writing style. This sentence offers an example of this: I could have written about students 'who happily use lots of different and often quite impressive words so as to say exactly what they mean, which in turn allows them to create a good argument', but I know that it is better to use the word 'articulate'.
- **Highfalutin words that few readers would understand**: This is a terrible temptation if you feel nervous about what you are trying to say, or anxious about how your readers are likely to respond. If I had given in to this temptation in the example above I might have said that students can be verbose in seminars, or garrulous, or loquacious. I very much like all of these words, but this guide is likely to have a wide readership and I would hate to put off any reader by a word which is unfamiliar.

Top Tip

I have known writers to become so anxious about what they perceive to be a narrow vocabulary that they look up new words to use, words which they have never heard or used before and never seen in context, in the hope that this will impress the reader. I did this just now through an online search engine and found 'multiloquent'. I have never heard of the word before and spellcheck dislikes it, but it does seem to be a word I could have chosen to replace 'articulate'. Try not to fall into this trap: you risk looking either elitist or foolish, or both.

- **Jargon which is too specific to your immediate group**: These are words which are used amongst experts in your field but which would not be familiar to a wider readership. Note that this wider group of readers could share your specialism but consist of readers who do not work alongside you in your institution or department. So, for example, at my university we would talk quite happily of 'overlap' when referring to the problem of students using material in assessed essays which they then reused in their exams. It was a decade before I heard the phrase 'double credit' to refer to exactly the same problem. You will not spot these problem words easily yourself, so make sure that a supporter who does not study or work in your organisation reviews your final document, looking particularly for such words.

- **Pompous words**: Words such as 'persons' for 'people', 'myself' for 'me' and 'proceed' for 'go' tend to irritate readers and so should be avoided. The rule of thumb here is that if you would be happy to use a word if you were in a formal academic discussion via email with your supervisor or mentor, or in a professional meeting giving a presentation, you can be fairly sure that the word is acceptable in a dissertation or report.

- **Slang words**: You will already know to avoid these, but you might want, again, to ask a critical friend to make sure that you have not slipped into slang (colloquialisms) by mistake. Sometimes what seems to you to be perfectly normal will seem too informal to other people. This is not about a static language: English is developing all the time and it should be, but it is not a good idea to use words which are on the cusp of turning from colloquial to formal at the risk of the word jarring on a reader's nerves.

- **Contracted words**: Having considered how challenging it can be to maintain a formal tone when language changes so much over time, we can move on to a much more simple issue: the contraction of words. By this I mean abbreviations such a 'couldn't', 'don't', 'we've', 'you'll' and 'aren't'. I would argue against the regular use of contractions such as these in your formal writing, for two reasons. First, by avoiding contractions you are reminding yourself throughout that this is a formal piece of work and should be written well. Second, although you might think that contractions make your writing accessible and friendly, there is a danger that others will find it slovenly and too casual. For the sake of simply writing out words in full, it is not worth the risk of offending or repelling even one reader.

American or British English?

Generally speaking, I would encourage the use of British English in a document originating in Britain, partly because this is what people would expect and partly because there will undoubtedly be readers who are irritated by seeing 'color' or 'maneuver' or other US spellings in documents which they took to be British in origin.

There are a few things to note about the use of British English:

Spelling: Spellcheck will default sometimes to English (US) rather than English (UK), usually if a document or part of a document has been downloaded and, occasionally, if your document has been sent around for review through an email system which has English (US) as a default. It can be surprisingly difficult to ensure that your system for that document reverts back to English (UK) and stays there.

Dates: It is always essential to include dates in any document with the month written as a whole word (8 June 2013) rather than as a number (8/6/13 or 08/06/13) because an American reader would assume you mean the 6th of August rather than the 8th of June. You might have noticed in the bracketed date above that I did not include the 'th' as a superscript after '8'. This is a more American way to produce figures in dates; indeed, in American English one would have '08 June 2013'. Although this might seem alien to the way you have always produced dates, it does produce a clearer, more easily read date and it is the industry standard for recording dates in many professional areas.

Top Tip

If you object to the idea of 08 June 2013, that is fine, but avoid using the argument 'but that is not how you say it; you say 8th June so it should have the 'th' superscript'. In fact, you say 'the 8th of June' and you will probably never have written it in that way so the argument is moot for most people.

Active/passive voice: There is one other potential exception to my urging the use of British English and it is about your style of writing. American writers tend to be enthusiastic about the active voice; generally, the British tend to prefer the passive. This can become a complicated issue, but one sentence will suffice to show the most basic difference between the two:

i. 'Monty reads the report'
ii. 'The report was read by Monty'

These two sentences are, for most purposes, the same sentence. They convey the same information and there is no deviation, except for the fact that the first is an active sentence and the second is a passive sentence:

1. **Monty** (called the subject of the sentence, the most important thing/person in the sentence) ... **reads** (this is a verb, a doing word, and it is in its active, simplest form) ... **the report** (the object of the sentence, the less important thing which is being acted upon by Monty). This is the active version of the sentence.
2. **The report** (this time, the report comes first) ... **was read by** (a passive verb, which is longer than its active counterpart) ... **Monty** (Monty comes last in the passive voice).

A report or dissertation written in American English style would have plenty of active voice sentences; these tend to be simpler and dynamic, more of a call to action. This might lead to a series of active sentences such as:

1. I inspected the site. It is contaminated. You will need to pay £63,000 to decontaminate it.

British English style tends to favour the passive, which is less direct and a little more deferential. In the passive voice the sentences would read:

2. The site was inspected by me. It was found that the site was contaminated. The cost of fixing the site will be a payment of £63,000 by you.

For most of the time you will write as you feel it should be written and will not worry about the active or the passive voice. If you do need to consider it, you will find that it can seem more difficult than the simple examples I have offered here, but the basic principles are no more complicated than these examples demonstrate.

You will have spotted that the passive sentences above are more distant in tone and longer than the active sentences, and this is the only basis on which I would encourage writers to consider altering their natural style. If you are always exceeding a word count, if you feel that your writing is rather long-winded, if nobody seems keen to read your writing, or takes notice and acts upon what you write, then I would suggest bringing some of your sentences into the active voice. Other than those circumstances, you can happily ignore this issue and simply write as you feel comes naturally.

Top Tip

One last word on tenses: generally, the present tense has more potential for impact. So, for example, you might choose to write 'we inspected the site six weeks ago and it is contaminated' rather than 'we inspected the site six weeks ago and it was contaminated'. Purists would tell you that the first version is the accurate statement anyway, but for the most part you will only need to consider this if you feel that you are not making your point forcefully enough in your writing.

Whose words?

The correct way to quote tends to trip writers up from time to time; if this is the case for you, there is probably good reason for it. School and college pupils are frequently told to italicise the words in a quotation, so it comes as a surprise to learn at university that this is not the standard way to quote. Journal and book publishers will often have their own rules about how to structure and punctuate quotations, which can leave you more confused. Added to this, there are several different academic and professional body style guides, not all of which agree on this issue, and your own organisation might have a house style guide or departmental handbook which differs again.

Top Tip

It can be disheartening to find yourself being offered several conflicting pieces of advice, with a book like this recommending one way, and you perhaps recalling being taught to do the same thing another way, and then a house style which suggests yet another way. Under these circumstances, follow the style guide under which the document is being written (an academic department's style guide or an organisation's house style guide) as these take precedence, even if you are not entirely convinced that they produce the best outcome.

Although, as the top tip above confirms, you will have to follow the style guide under which you writing, if you are not offered guidance or directives, you could follow the conventions offered here.

If you have chosen a quotation of fewer than about 2–3 lines, you can simply include it in the sentence with nothing more than single inverted commas around it:

> According to the fire safety handbook that I read recently, in the event of fire, 'regardless of how the fire started and, in most cases, irrespective of whether the fire is chemical or electrical as each of these is possible', you must use the fire extinguisher marked D2 in the lobby.

If you are leaving some words out of your quotation, you would replace them with an ellipsis (...) and if you want to add a few words you would put them in square brackets to show that they are your own. For example:

> According to the fire safety handbook that I read recently, in the event of fire, 'regardless of how the fire started ... irrespective of whether the fire is chemical or electrical as each of these is [more than] possible', you must use the fire extinguisher marked D2 in the lobby.

There is no colon (:) or semi-colon (;) used to introduce this quotation; there is no need. The idea is that the quotation should fit perfectly into what you are saying and so does not need any punctuation to introduce it. A semi-colon would always be inaccurate in this situation (more on semi-colons later) and if you feel the urge to include a colon even though you know that it is not needed for this type of quotation, you might consider whether your quotation is a little long and would be better laid out as a lengthy quotation.

Lengthy quotations (those of more than two or three lines) would usually be placed down a page:

> This is a fake quotation which I am using to illustrate the layout of lengthy quotations; brief quotations, unlike their longer counterparts, simply flow along a line with single inverted commas at either end of them. It is interesting to note that longer quotations are indented but are not enclosed by inverted commas.

Quotations from verse sections of plays will be laid out in the same way as any poetry quote that runs down the page. Thus, for example, you might write the following:

> Shakespeare reflects Oberon's royal status when he speaks in verse to Puck:

> I know a bank where the wild thyme blows,

> Where oxlips and the nodding violet grows,

> Quite over-canopied with the luscious woodbine,

> With sweet musk-roses and with eglantine:

> Where Titania sleeps... (Act 2, Scene I, ll. 248–253)

Similarly with poetry, as in the following:

> Donne's frequent use of the explosive 'b' sound to open his poems lends a dynamic quality to his writing:

> Blasted with sighs, and surrounded with teares,

> Hither I come to seeke the spring,

> And at mine eyes, and at mine eares,

> Receive such balmes, as else cure every thing;

> Within 'Twicknam Garden', quoted above, the heavy use of punctuation combines with this forceful opening to arrest the reader's attention and stress the speaker's pain.

You will notice that the whole quotations are indented, and that there are three full stops (the ellipsis again) at the end of the Shakespeare quotation to indicate that I have omitted part of that line. These are taken from very old editions of the texts, and so might differ in punctuation from more modern editions. It is important that you use the punctuation, spelling and format of your quotation exactly as in the source material that you are using, rather than being tempted to change the punctuation to make it more in keeping with your own writing style.

Top Tip

The title of an item which has been published as an entity in itself (such as a book, a report or a lengthy poem) is given in italics; other items (single chapters in books, shorter poems and so forth) are given in unitalicised text enclosed by single inverted commas (single quotation marks).

Types of words and what they do

'Parts of speech' is the term used to categorise the building blocks, such as words, which make up our language. Knowledge of them is, of course, essential to a grammarian or someone who is learning a language; for the rest of us, as we write this is much less important. You know the language well enough to be writing a dissertation or report in that language and so your use of English will be at a level where you will not be pausing over each word, trying to create a sentence. However, if you are told by a supporter, mentor or colleague that your use of adverbs is awkward, it can be embarrassing to have to ask what an adverb is. So, I am offering you here the most basic of definitions of the parts of speech which are most relevant to an everyday discussion of writing.

Top Tip

The definitions I am about to give you are not exhaustive. They are a brief, useful outline of each definition to show you how these words work; if you come to explore them further you will, inevitably, find far more complex definitions for each.

A noun: is the name of something (**building, river, woman**) which is general rather than specific.

A proper noun: is the 'proper name' of a specific thing or person (**Albert Hall, River Thames, Sophia**).

Top Tip

It is usually easiest to stick to the rule of thumb that proper nouns have capital letters at the beginning of the word. So, Delphinium would take a capital letter at the beginning if it was the name of a little girl, but would not if it was just the name of a flower.

A pronoun: usually stands in for a noun, such as **you**, **that**, **it**, **he**.

An adjective: describes or changes/adds to the basic meaning of a noun (**large** building, **wide** river, **tall** woman, **regal** Albert Hall, **mighty** River Thames, **beautiful** Sophia).

A verb: is often called 'a doing word'; it is a word or phrase which describes an action (**run, jump, walk, writing, has written, going to eat, will eat**).

Top Tip

Calling a verb a 'doing word' causes all sorts of confusion because, as you will just have seen, it can be made up of several words. Each of the words in such phrases will have its own description as a part of speech, but we need not concern ourselves with that here.

An adverb: describes or changes/adds to the meaning of any word of phrase which can be described or changed/added to, with the exception of nouns. In most cases we tend to think of adverbs as acting upon verbs, probably because the term 'adverb' seems to imply this. Adverbs do act upon verbs (she walked **slowly**) but they can also affect words which are not verbs (you are **quite** right, I did see her walking; we could have been walking **together**).

Top Tip

Adverbs can be tricky because they are used in so many different ways. For the purposes of your writing, it is the adverb ending in 'ly' that you will need to watch most closely. If you use this type of adverb too often, it can either reduce the power of your argument (**possibly, presumably, unlikely**) or make it seems as if you are blustering, perhaps even lying (**absolutely, undeniably, indubitably**). It is a relief to know that we only tend to overuse adverbs in this way when we are nervous or unsure of our case, so if you have planned well and feel confidence in your argument you can avoid this problem.

A preposition: as its name implies, this is a word which shows the position in which something has been before now (pre-position) or where something is at the moment, or to whence it is going. Prepositions include words such as **to, from, by, of, over, under, in, into, on, onto, with, within**.

Top Tip

You might have spotted the word 'whence' in the definition of prepositions above. This word exists as a result of prepositions. I was taught at school that you should never end a sentence with a preposition, so I would say **'to whence it is going'** rather than **'where it is going to'** because 'to' on the end of a sentence would sound strange to me. I realise that this rule of English can seem dated nowadays but it should not be forgotten altogether. If you are told that your writing is rather gawky in style, that it reads more like spoken than formal, written English, check the ends of your sentences. If you often end them with a preposition it is a clear sign that you did not think through your sentence before you started to write it.

Top Tip

'On'/'onto' and 'in'/'into' are not interchangeable and often worry writers. If you are not sure which one to use, decide first whether the 'to' links to the word after it (which, if it does, should be a verb). If this is the case, then you split apart the 'on' and 'to' or the 'in' and 'to'. You would write **'I came into the room'** or **'I came to talk to you'**; **'I got onto the bus'** or **'I got on to make my journey easier'**.

A note on clauses: loosely speaking, clauses are groups of words which then make up sentences. There are many different types of clause, but the two that you may come across and which are most useful for you to recognise are a **main clause**, which can make a whole sentence in itself ('**My boss loved the report**'), and a **subordinate clause**, which attaches to a main clause either before it ('**Despite all of my fears, my boss loved my report**') or after it ('**My boss loved the report despite my fears**') or within it ('**My boss, despite all my fears, loved the report**').

Whole words?

Although we use complete words most of the time, there are occasions when we might choose to use an abbreviated form of a phrase, giving the initial letters of most or all of the words in the phrase instead. If the abbreviation this produces is just a string of letters it is usually called an '**initialism**' (the **BBC**); if the abbreviation makes a recognisable word it will usually be called an '**acronym**' (a **SWOT** analysis). However, many people will always just use one of the terms, or use them interchangeably.

The letters in an abbreviation will commonly be taken from the first letters of only the important words in the initial phrase, but they are sometimes taken from all the letters, or from most of the letters in the whole phrase (including minor words such as 'a', 'of', 'the') if this helps to create an acronym rather than an initialism. Sometimes, indeed, whole sections of words are extracted from the original phrase and then put together to form an abbreviation. There are several guidelines you will need to follow when using abbreviations:

- There was a time when the letters in abbreviations were separated by full stops (the **B.B.C.)** but this looks a little old-fashioned now: it is more elegant to dispense with them (the **BBC**). If you prefer to keep them, make sure that you do put full stops all the way through. It is easy to miss one out to odd effect. Writing '**an A.B.T.A travel agent**' could leave the reader wondering if you missed out the full stop at the end of an abbreviation or whether you missed out a space between sentences. The reader might then try out '**an A.B.T. A travel agent**', realise that makes no sense and go back, rereading the phrase as '**an ABTA travel agent**'. The reader will probably get there in the end, but will have had to waste time.
- If you are using an abbreviation which is already in circulation, you should reproduce it exactly as you have seen it in general use. This issue arises most commonly when an organisation brands itself using lower case letters for an acronym, or takes an odd assortment of letters from different parts of its name in order to make an abbreviation. Although you might be able to think of a more grammatically correct way to present the abbreviation, you will have to accept it as it is.
- There are two ways in which you might reveal to the reader the original phrase from which you are taking the acronym. You could give the whole phrase first, followed by the abbreviation in brackets afterwards: **The European Court of Justice (ECJ)**; alternatively, you might prefer to place the abbreviation first, followed by the full term: **ECJ (European Court of Justice)**. The first is more usual, and, in my view, easier on the reader. Note that just because you are about to give an abbreviation in capital letters, there is no need to capitalise the first letters of the original words unless you would normally do so. If you wanted, for example, to abbreviate **early day closing** to **EDC** that is how you would show it (not **Early Day Closing**).
- It used to be standard advice to give the term in full and its abbreviation just once in a document, the first time that you used the abbreviation. This convention is less strictly

observed now and the focus is more on being helpful to your reader. If, for example, you use the abbreviation several times and then you do not use it for six pages, but you have a section break within those pages, you might choose to show the full term again prior to the next use of the abbreviation, especially if you are aware that many of your readers are likely to be reading selected sections of your report rather than the report in its entirety.

Top Tip

Make sure that you *always* give the term in full when you use an abbreviation (in reports, this needs to be done both in the text itself and in a glossary or list of abbreviations). You will have seen an example of this earlier on in this section on abbreviations. I referred three times to the BBC without telling you what the acronym meant. I could assume that you knew that I was referring to the British Broadcasting Corporation, which is the most common use of this initialism. However, you could have presumed that I meant Bristol Borough Council, or Birmingham Bus Company. In this context it did not matter, but in another document it might have ruined your understanding of my point completely.

- The choice between putting 'a' or 'an' before an abbreviation can be problematic if you are unsure of the rule about the use of these words. You may never have given it much thought, but you are probably happy to follow the rule of putting 'an' before a word which begins with a vowel (**a, e, i, o, u**) and 'a' before words beginning with any other letter (these are called consonants). However, this rule is one of only a few in the everyday use of English which relies on how the word sounds, not how it looks on the page. You will already be following this rule without any great thought in cases such as **a uniform approach** because the sound at the beginning of 'uniform' is actually 'y', even though it is a vowel on the page. The only time this seems to muddle writers is when you have a consonant on the page but it is actually a vowel sound because it is an initial. The police might refer to 'an RTA' for **'a road traffic accident'** because 'R' begins with an 'a' sound when you read it aloud and this is how it should be written.

Exploring so many aspects of abbreviations with you reflects their importance in our writing. They are certainly very useful tools in many ways. However, they can also be extremely detrimental to your writing style. If you use them in a way that is not helpful for the reader, you will simply alienate that reader, who will not want to read past your first misuse of an abbreviation. There are several uses to avoid:

1. If you are only using an abbreviation once or twice there is no point in abbreviating the longer phrase unless (like the BBC example) you are sure that all of your readers would expect the phrase to be abbreviated.

2. Try to avoid abbreviations in titles and headings. They can look awkward and you will, presumably, be using the full term within a short space.
3. Never refer the reader to an online glossary on your organisation's intranet; this would be useless to any external reader.
4. Be aware that any abbreviation you use might already be in use elsewhere with another root phrase. If you have just made up an acronym for one document and you have a glossary, you might want to include in the glossary (or list of abbreviations) a section entitled 'Report abbreviations' or 'Dissertation abbreviations' meaning that this is a list of abbreviations you have chosen to make up yourself and the reader should be aware that they might not appear in this form anywhere else.
5. If you find yourself using abbreviations all the time, can hardly get through a sentence without one, tend to talk in abbreviations or feel far more important whenever you use an abbreviation … just stop using them (or at least cut down by 70 per cent on the amount you use).

Top Tip

Some publishers, commercial organisations and academic departments now tend to frown on the use of e.g., i.e., etc., even on the more modern version of eg, ie, etc. Indeed, some publishing houses will require the use of the full terms (such as 'for example' for 'e.g.', 'that is' for 'i.e.', 'and so forth' for 'etc'). It seems alien when first you come to write in this way, but I have found that it has a beneficial effect in that it makes me consider more carefully whether I needed to use these abbreviations as much as I always had; I came to see that I had been casually overusing them and am pleased to have been called to account.

New words?

We tend to think of hyphens as stable in their use and not subject to change over time, but this is a misconception. (A hyphen is the little line that joins two parts of a word together, such as in sub-strata.) The example I have just given demonstrates perfectly the way in which we really use hyphens and why they are subject to change. One of the reasons (and there are many) why English is such a rich and nuanced language is because of the way in which our language structure allows us to make up words whenever it suits us, and we often use hyphens to do this.

Although we tend not to notice hyphens particularly, we would not expect today to see '**house-wife**', '**drive-way**' or '**to-morrow**' as words containing hyphens, but they once did, along with very many of our commonly used words. It is one of the great things about the language, but it also leads to confusion from time to time. The word **sub-strata**: should it be two words with no hyphen? Should it be two words with no attempt to join them with a hyphen? Should it be one word? A search engine has just offered me a variety of webpages that display the use of every one of these options, which has confirmed my hunch that this is a word on the move.

Writers choose to place two words together and connect them with a hyphen because they believe that the use of the words is improved if they are read as one word. Over time, as with the example above, the words might become single words in common usage and in our dictionaries. 'Substrata' will settle down in the end into one word. In some cases the attempt to join fails. I was reading a novel from the 1950s the other day and '**tea-party**' was hyphenated. You would not expect to see this as one word, or even as a hyphenated phrase now, largely because we stopped having so many tea parties. There are other attempts to hyphenation that fail repeatedly. '**Thank you**' is a good example of this. It occasionally appears on notices with a hyphen (thank-you) or as one word (thankyou) but is unlikely ever to become one word.

The problem for most writers is that hyphens can catch you out. If you are told (even by a trusted supervisor or mentor) that a word has a hyphen in the middle, joining two parts of the word, and you feel sure that you are used to seeing it as one word, go back and check before you assume you need to change it. It is the one piece of punctuation which tends to link to age: the older you are, the more likely you are to be including hyphens which have disappeared.

Top Tip

If you find yourself in the irritating position of meaning to use a dash (a dash is a long line – with a space on either side) and instead you keep being offered a hyphen (a smaller line, with no space either side) you might wonder why it is happening. You might even insert spaces either side of the hyphen in the hope that this will make it better, but it just makes it look even odder. This is happening because of the way that your word processing software works. It will only give you a dash if you type a word, then a space, then press the 'hyphen/dash' key, then another space, then a word, then a third space. Only at this third space will your hyphen suddenly and satisfyingly spring open to form a long dash. If, at any stage in this process, you move away from the point at which you are typing, the default system will not work.

Just one example of words with which I struggle because of a hyphen is the word 'coordinated'. Spellcheck is happy for me to use it without a hyphen, but then it also lets me use it with a hyphen (co-ordinated). My students would look askance at me for trying to insert the hyphen, so I have to make a decision to look a little old fashioned in my writing but stick with what is familiar, or to move with the times and use 'coordinated'. I recall when e-mail had a firm hyphen in the middle, yet I know now that it has segued, as it should, into 'email' in most of the writing one sees.

This has to be a conscious choice and I would suggest that, as the introduction and then the loss of hyphens is a continuous process that has given us such an interesting language, it is best to accept progress as hyphens disappear: there will always be an intriguing new word just around the corner. Of course, you might be the next person to put two words together in this way and, in a few years' time, you might see your word, unhyphenated, in the dictionary.

There is another use of hyphens that was once a firm rule of English which I notice has softened in recent times. The rule was that if you had two words which should be read together in order to describe the next word in a sentence (an example of one type of **adjectival phrase**), the describing words would be joined by a hyphen. So, you could write that you are interested in **film making**, or that you are interested in **film-making techniques**. You might work **part time**, and that would make you a **part-time worker**. In each of these examples the hyphen is used to show that you are describing a later word in the sentence ('England' and 'worker'). This was, for some readers, a useful indication of what was meant; for others, it seemed to be an irritation ('I can read a few words and work out how they go together, so why include it?'). It could also lead to some slight clumsiness if you wanted to write, for example, 'Is this a full- or part-time position?', a sentence in which the hyphens show that both 'full' and 'part' are connected to the word 'time'. It might be for these reasons that this rule seems to have become more of a convention and is ignored by many writers for most of the time.

I am an enthusiastic supporter of the rules of English and so would not be the type of person who would abandon a rule or even a convention lightly, but in this case I can see that it can work well to do this. There is an ease to 'film making techniques' which is perhaps missing from 'film-making techniques'. Purists might disagree with this viewpoint entirely, but that is why this is not a standard book on grammar. I am keen for your writing to be both impressive and effective and so want to let you know which rules are absolute and which might be changing even as you read this. Generally, the rules change slowly and relatively rarely, so you can feel secure in your language despite developments in it over time.

There is one final example of the use of a hyphen which is still relevant and which could save you embarrassment and/or confusion. If I were to go to my gym after a break of a few weeks I might want to work out using several of the machines so as to try to make up for my absence, so I would bounce into the gym and jump on my cross-trainer. Why the hyphen? Because I want to make it clear that, despite the fact that my trainer would be angry with me for missing so many gym sessions, I did not jump on him, **my cross trainer**, but rather on the exercise machine, **my cross-trainer**. These glitches in meaning are not always easy to spot when you are writing, but they can easily confuse or amuse you when you read it back, especially if you are in the habit of reading aloud to yourself, and then you will be reaching for a hyphen to spare any confusion.

Top Tip

Despite the richness of our language we can still be tempted to include Latinate forms from time to time. A popular Latin phrase at the moment seems to be '**inter alia**' (meaning 'amongst other things'). The first time one reads this in an email amongst colleagues it can be a pleasant, momentary diversion from English. By time number six in a single day it is setting one's teeth on edge. Only use a term from another language if you are absolutely sure of its meaning and if you feel it adds something special to a sentence in a way that an English term could not. If you expect your readers to understand it, then there is no need to use italics to highlight how daring you are being: just include it as if it were any other word.

I could not hope, nor did I intend, to offer you a comprehensive guide to all aspects of words in this chapter. What I hope to have achieved with you, though, is a shared sense of the importance of using the right word in its context and an agreed understanding of some of the most relevant rules relating to words for dissertation and report writers. You may once have known these rules, you may never have been taught them, but now you can move ahead with the writing phase of your report or dissertation with confidence that you will not trip yourself up over basic errors. As I have covered the most common mistakes I find again and again in writing that I assess, I know that I have given you the most immediate and relevant help: you are now ready to move with me on to the rather briefer topic of phrases.

19

Phrases

The fashion of phrases

You will now be aware, from our consideration of words, that language changes over time. There is nothing necessarily wrong with projecting an image of old-fashioned gravitas (much as I just did with the hyphen in that sentence, some might argue), but you do need to be aware that this is what you are doing. You also need to be as sure as you reasonably can be that you will not be irritating your readers. There are two particular types of phrase I want to ponder with you in this context: the use of singular/plural and the overuse of clichés.

Writers, because they want their writing to flow smoothly, are often tempted to avoid the minor awkwardness of the phrase 'he or she', or the more streamlined equivalents 'he/she' or 's/he'. The way writers might do this is to use phrases which do not make sense in their context, by swinging from singular to plural in a sentence. Examples would include 'the reader will find that they enjoy this book immensely' and 'the user will enjoy it when they try this software'. In both of these cases, the writer clearly felt awkward about writing 'he or she' and so opted, perhaps without much thought, for the plural later in the sentence, having started off with a singular 'reader' and 'user'.

The hapless writer will be completely unaware of the significant problem that this tiny choice will have caused. Many readers loathe this incorrect phrasing. 'Why?' they shout. 'Surely you can see that you have started off with a singular person, so how can that person suddenly have transformed into a crowd of people within just a few words?' This outraged response is no exaggeration: I have seen it many times. Luckily, it is a problem which is easy to fix once you are aware that have developed this habit. Simply change the singular person to a plural group in the earlier part of the sentence: **readers will find that they enjoy this book immensely** and **users will enjoy this software when**

they try it. There are few cases where this approach will not work and, if you come across one of them, it is better to use 'he or she' or an equivalent later in the sentence than risk the response that this oversight can cause.

Clichés are phrases which go in and out of fashion. They are rarely more than five or six words long and they never add to a sentence in any meaningful way. Moreover, they can make your writing style pompous, vacuous and slightly comic. Clichés which I am spotting at the moment include **in point of fact** and **to be fair**; some years ago it was **blue sky thinking**, **out of the box** and **in point of fact**; the next trend coming up is likely to be **tick all the boxes**, **drill down into the situation** and **a blank canvas**. Some clichés are a perennial problem; these include **at this moment in time** and **at the end of the day**.

If you are not sure what is fashionable in clichés at the moment, take a look at any reality television programme or popular sports channel: that is often where the fashion begins. The way to deal with them is straightforward: recognise them in our language, spot them in your writing and firmly, without any qualms, delete them forever.

The folly of phrases

We can all lapse, from time to time, into using 'personal ticks' in our writing, little phrases which we are drawn to use repeatedly, sometimes with no awareness that we are using them. Indeed, they are sometimes phrases which we despise and would not expect to use under any circumstances, yet they creep into our writing. These are not like clichés, which you might mistakenly think are useful additions to a sentence, but rather phrases such as **as it were**, **in recent times**, **and furthermore**, **at a basic level**, **in and of itself**, **without preamble** and similar. They are not necessarily wrong in themselves; a little too vague perhaps and not adding much meaning, and their occasional use might add something to a sentence. They also tend to run with fashion. A few years ago **for sure** crept into several reports I read and nowadays, as one could have predicted, phrases using **like** are stealing into our writing (as in, **it is like the whole project is going to fail if we miss this deadline**).

Repeated use of these phrases will have detrimental effects:

1. Your writing will become less focused and your writing voice less commanding.
2. Your readers will be slightly distracted, wondering why you are using the phrase and looking out for its next use, noticing it every time you use it at the expense of the points you are actually trying to make.
3. If your repetition becomes very noticeable, readers might be amused by what you are doing and look out for the phrase with a wry smile. Again, this is not a response you will want to elicit.

I would not argue for a moment that all small, peripheral phrases are in this category. Many such phrases are useful. For example, I would support the use of **it is both** (as in, **it is both cost effective and beneficial**) as this suggests that you are being judicious and weighing up both sides of the argument. It is also, in this context, a signposting phrase which helps the reader to grasp the sentence and so would increase the impact of that sentence.

Your challenge with respect to these phrases is therefore twofold: you need to use any phrase which you can see is adding something to the meaning of the sentence, or is helping the reader to understand what you are saying, or is making a positive contribution to your writing style. You then need to eradicate from your writing those personal ticks which are not helping you to express yourself well.

Top Tip

It can be very difficult to spot these ticks, even when you read your writing through to yourself. I recently wrote a three page-long document and used the phrase 'in recent years' four times. I had no idea that I had done it and was very grateful when a colleague pointed out the error. You could ask a friend or supporter to look at your writing to spot these ticks. You will need probably 6–8 pages of writing and the phrases will jump out at them straight away. You can then make a note of each phrase and stick it by your computer screen until you know you are cured of the habit.

20

Sentences

How long is the perfect sentence?

There is an unhelpful answer to this: however long you need it to be. There are also answers which are intended to be useful, but which give you precise word counts and so become useless as soon as you try to express something very simple or exceedingly complex. I will try here to offer you some rather more productive guidelines.

I was taught in school that most of the sentences I wrote should be 12–25 words long. This is not a bad guideline, as long as you are prepared to have some longer sentences when you need them and some much, much shorter sentences when you want to create punchy impact. Sentence length is all about variety: because different lengths of sentences have different effects, you can use this to your advantage. Short, snappy little sentences of, say, 6–8 words will make your points very clearly. If introduced into a series of longer sentences, a short sentence like this can also add impact. However, if you only write in short sentences your writing will become monotonous and strangely child-like.

A series of short sentences is not exciting:

The test material was placed under the microscope. This was done in sterile conditions. The damaged cells became obvious. They covered 24.3% of the observable area. The stain increased their visibility under these conditions. This was the first test sample. We have five more to examine. These have been provided by our six sponsor organisations. This can only be done if there is lab time available. This might be an issue next month. Looking for new facilities would help with this.

... adding even one longer sentence can make it more interesting and easier to grasp:

> The test material was placed under the microscope in sterile conditions and the damaged cells, covering 24.3% of the observable area, became obvious. The stain increased their visibility under these conditions. This was the first test sample. We have five more to examine. These have been provided by our six sponsor organisations. This can only be done if there is lab time available. This might be an issue next month. Looking for new facilities would help with this.

Relying throughout on longer sentences makes the writing flow well:

> The test material was placed under the microscope in sterile conditions and the damaged cells became obvious. They covered 24.3% of the observable area, the stain making them more visible. This was the first of six samples provided by our sponsors to be tested. This can only be done if there is lab time available, which might be an issue next month. Looking for new facilities would help with this.

... but sentences which are too long can be inaccessible:

> The test material was placed under the microscope in sterile conditions and the damaged cells, made more obvious by the stain, were seen to cover 24.3% of the observable area; however, we have five more samples to examine (all samples being provided by our sponsors) and we need enough lab time, which has necessitated the consideration of a move to new facilities next month.

... including a short sentence can make it easier for the reader to grasp:

> The test material was placed under the microscope in sterile conditions and the damaged cells, made more obvious by the stain, were seen to cover 24.3% of the observable area. Our sponsors have provided six samples. In order to examine them all we need enough lab time, so we must consider a move to new facilities next month.

The effect of sentence length is felt more strongly at the lengthier end of the scale than at the shorter, so as soon as about a third of your sentences are more than 25 words long your reader will start to feel the strain a little, finding your writing slightly rambling and dense. At the other end of the scale, it would not be until about two-thirds of your sentences were fewer than 12 words that your reader would start to be bothered by the note-like quality of your writing.

Inexperienced writers are sometimes encouraged to write in short sentences so as to avoid the problem of rambling, and also on the false assumption that they will make fewer punctuation mistakes if they use shorter sentences. It is hard to be persuasive if your writing is a series of brief sentences, so I would rather persuade you to use a variety of sentence lengths rather than sticking to the apparent safety of the short sentence. Of course, this discussion relies on you knowing how long your sentences tend to be, and surprisingly few writers ever think to check this. You will need about three pages of your writing to get an accurate count on this. Count up the number of words in the first sentence and jot it down, then keep going until you have a tally of all the sentence lengths in those few pages. The pattern created by this list of numbers will be individual to your style and will differ depending on whether you are writing formally or more casually. If most of your sentences are in the 12–25 word range, you will know that you have a steady and easily accessible writing style. If a small proportion of your sentences have a word count outside this range, you will know that you are adding verve to your writing style. If the majority of your sentences are outside this range, you need to examine whether you should begin to work on a more useful sentence length.

Top Tip

It is a bit fiddly to work through your writing, counting up words, but doing this even once could be a revelation to you. Once you have discovered your range, you might want to make a note of it and check it every six or nine months to see whether it has moved. In between word counting checks, you can set up your spellcheck to give you 'readability statistics' in a text box. This will give you all sorts of interesting details, such as the average number of words per sentence, so it is a useful tool to gauge your overall writing style, although you will still need to do the detailed count from time to time.

Starting a sentence

It seems obvious at first thought: you start a sentence in writing just as you would in speech, whenever you want to start on your next thought, the next thing you want to say. This approach will work well for you in your writing, but you can see from the example about sentence length that you have choices about whether you start a new sentence at all: you might include a piece of punctuation (as I have done again in this sentence) so as to make your writing more flowing and persuasive. By doing this my writing is more likely to feel like part of a conversation we are having, rather than a treatise on writing style, so you will want to use this in your writing.

Even experienced writers can have blind spots about some aspects of punctuation, so I have included a discussion in Part Six ('Polishing') that explores how punctuation can be used to increase the impact of your sentences. There is no need to force this: it will come to you naturally as your command of, and confidence in, your use of punctuation grows.

There are no rules (beyond using a capital letter) about the beginning of a sentence, but there are words that you might want to avoid. Schoolchildren are often taught that they should never begin a sentence with the words 'and' or 'but' and should opt instead to use 'also' or 'in addition' in place of 'and' and 'however' or 'nevertheless' rather than 'but'. Although arguments rage amongst academics about whether or not it is good style to avoid certain words at the beginning of sentences (and other words do join 'and' and 'but' in this debate from time to time), you can take a pragmatic approach. As you are likely to irritate or distract some of your readers by beginning a sentence with either of these words, and given that you have other words at your disposal which will do the same job, you can simply avoid using them in this position.

Top Tip

The use of capital letters at the beginning of words seems to be causing anxiety at the moment. They are used, as you will know, at the beginning of sentences. They are usually used throughout an acronym or initialism. They are used at the beginning of a legally defined term in a legal document (but not elsewhere: 'client' only has a capital 'C' if it is being used as a legally defined term). They are also used for proper nouns (names of people, places, projects and so forth). Beyond these categories, only use a capital letter at the beginning of a word if you have very good reason to; if you have any doubts, check before you capitalise.

Finishing a sentence

When you have completed writing down a thought you will, for the most part, instinctively put a full stop and move to the next sentence. The length of your sentences may change depending on what you are trying to achieve, and your sentence length may also change over time. If you want to create a different effect from your sentence length, you will do this most easily when you come to check your report or dissertation.

Top Tip

Sometimes, less experienced writers produce 'run-on sentences'. This is done by putting a comma where a full-stop should be, so that two sentences are awkwardly and incorrectly joined together. This is confusing for the reader, which is handy for you in trying to fix it. By reading your writing out loud you will spot these run-on sentences quite easily and will be able to fix them by replacing the comma with a full stop.

You need to make a distinction between the end of a sentence and the end of a paragraph. We will be looking at paragraphs in the next chapter, but here I want to remind you that a sentence is only ever followed by a space (or two spaces) without any pressing of the return key. It can sometimes be tempting to set your system up so that you have to press the return key twice in order to make a proper paragraph break; this gives you have the option of pressing it just once to create an odd break, not quite a paragraph break but somehow a little more than a full stop and a sentence break.

I have done this here to demonstrate how it works.

This is never a good idea: it makes your writing look indecisive and muddled. Readers will wonder why you have done it, which is a distraction you will not want to create, and it will also, over time, confuse your writing style.

Top Tip

You might habitually leave either one or two spaces between sentences and this is a matter of personal choice. In documents which contain an abundance of figures, formula and abbreviations, some might argue that two spaces is preferable as offering a little more rest for the eyes. As either usage is acceptable, there is no need to change your normal practice; you just need to be aware that if you are reviewing someone else's writing and they differ from you, they are not wrong.

21

Paragraphs

Paragraphs offer readers the mental space that they need to feel fully involved in your writing, so you ignore them at your peril. Having stated that so firmly, I want to consider with you why paragraphs go wrong, because they do, in all sorts of ways. The first way in which your use of paragraphs might begin to break down is when you ask yourself whether, in order to maintain your fluent style of writing, you really want to use them at all. You are breaking up your text in other ways, with section and/or chapter breaks, perhaps with illustrations or headings, maybe also with graphs, charts and tables. With so much already fracturing the text, should you add more?

The answer to this is a firm 'yes', and the reason rests with the word 'fracturing' that I used in the last sentence. All of the examples I just offered to you are insertions that you may be required to make because of the nature of your document and/or because of a house or organisational style guide you are expected to follow. They might feel at times as if they are fracturing your writing; paragraphs, on the other hand, are entirely under your control and you can use them to great effect.

Top Tip

I was taught in school that a paragraph should have an average of 3–4 sentences in it. This relied on my also noting the convention that sentences should be about 12–15 words long, but it seemed to work quite well, as long as I remembered to vary paragraph length occasionally, just as I would sentence length. An entirely mechanical approach to paragraphing could be detrimental to your style, given that paragraphs are about structuring the meaning of what you are trying to say rather than numbers of words, but this is still a useful guideline. Looking back through my writing here I am struck by how many of my paragraphs are still 3–4 sentences long.

How well you use paragraphs may depend on you taking a few minutes now to consider the effect that they have on your reader. More than any other tool in your armoury of writing, they are a clear visual and emotional stimulus to your reader; their use relies on the **'lazy Z' principle** which underpins our reading experience. It is one of many principles relating to why and how we read things in certain ways, and I will explain it here so that you can see how it might affect your choices on paragraphing.

When you come to read a document or view an image it is, just for a moment, an experience which makes you feel vulnerable. This will not usually be a conscious anxiety, but it will have an impact on how you respond. You may have noticed this if you have been in a seminar or meeting when a handout is passed around the room. As soon as it begins its circulation around a group, all those at the 'end of the line' of its progress will glance across at it as it comes around sometimes. This is a display of minor vulnerability which we, of course, ignore in ourselves and others as being of no great importance.

Top Tip

Now you know why, if you are giving a paper or presentation and you need to distribute a handout, it is best to do it at the outset or the end, or to leave ample time for it to circulate. If you start to refer to it in any way as it is circulating your audience will be upset.

This vulnerability is based on the purposes behind writing and reading. We know that, as readers, something will be asked of us when we encounter a document. We might be expected to do something as a result of reading it or, at the very least, we are expected to understand what is included in it. We do not notice we are feeling in this way because, before we have a chance to consider it, we are focusing on the details of the document.

Vulnerability is not always our uppermost response to a document or an image. If we are rushed for time, we might want to scan the page just to see if we want to read further (this is why career coaches put such stress on the visual impact of a CV); if we are being shown an advertising image, we will not be prepared to give it more than a few moments of our time; if we are in a meeting and expected to discuss a paper which is being circulated, we need to take in the salient information at speed and so our main emotional response might be a sense of urgency and, perhaps, a little irritation that we have not seen the document in advance; either way, we will be scanning it before we read it.

So, we have an emotional response to documents, and this can be linked effectively to our visual response to a series of paragraphs on the page.

In the document below, the writer has given up on paragraphs:

In this next document the writer has used several textual options, including paragraph breaks, a bullet-pointed list and a subheading:

Asldfkjasldj

When readers look at the first page in this example, their eyes will not, as you might logically expect, run from left to right on the page, starting from the beginning of the first line and then taking each line in turn, like this:

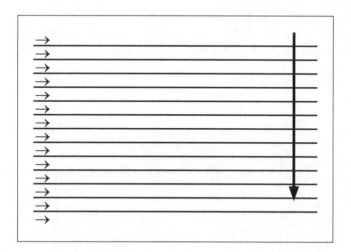

Rather than a logical path for viewing, readers will actually scan across the top of the page, then diagonally back across the whole of the page and then across on the vertical again to cover the very bottom of the page:

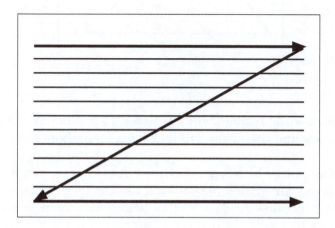

You can see from this illustration why this is referred to as the 'lazy Z' method of reading. Once readers have scanned in this way (and they will do this so fast and it will be so automatic to them that they will not be aware of doing it) they will read the document, but without any great enthusiasm. The lazy Z scan has shown them that there is not a single break on this page: no illustrations, charts or graphs, no headings or subheadings, no lists down the page or paragraphing to provide escape points.

In contrast to this, if a reader looks at my second example page, the experience will be quite different. The initial, lazy Z scan will take place in the same way:

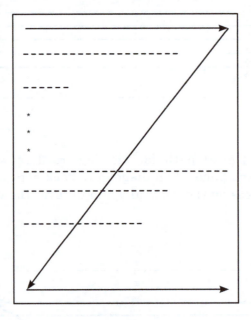

... but in this case the readers will have seen that there are distinctive features on the page and their eyes will flick back up to those features, confirming them.

This is a page with which readers will want to engage, and it is pages like this which make your writing appealing. I use the term 'engage' here, rather than just 'read', because readers will be doing more than just reading; you have given them breaks in the text such that they can escape from the writing

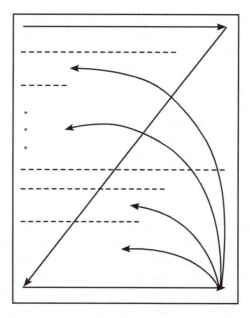

and take some time to ponder what you have asserted so far and to contemplate where you might go next. This is a far more productive way to read and it allows you to be a more successful writer, simply by virtue of some paragraph breaks.

Top Tip

Now that you know about the lazy Z, you might enjoy spotting it elsewhere. Advertisers, in particular, are adept at its use, so next time you look at a magazine advert draw a mental lazy Z across the page: the text and images, or parts of images, which fall along the lazy Z line are those that the advertisers especially want you to remember from the advertisement.

One question that is often asked is how many paragraphs should be included in a page of text? As I write this I am using Calibri size 12 font, single spaced, and I am including between four and six paragraph breaks per side of A4 (and I also have breaks for tops tips and lists). This is more than I would normally use: the ideal standard per page is often quoted as three to four breaks. My rather more frequent paragraphing here is not surprising, given that I am hoping to produce a text which is as accessible and easy to use as I can make it, whereas a report or dissertation is less likely to be structured as 'an easy read'. Not that everything I write needs to be easy.

The way in which this paragraph and the one above are structured in relation to each other demonstrates a common problem with paragraphing which you can avoid with practice. Having referred in the previous paragraph to trying to create an accessible, easy read, I then mentioned that this need not be the case for everything I write and so, naturally, you were expecting me to start this paragraph with an explanation of why a writer might not feel the need to make all of their writing easy to read. So where is the true break? The paragraph break we see is there, on the page, just before this paragraph, but it is not actually a break at all, because I began on the subject matter of this paragraph before the break: this is called a '**run-on paragraph**'.

We have seen the importance of summarising with the success of the mobile phone app which summarises web pages. For the busy browser, apps such as this are going to become increasingly important, but they rely on the ability of the website creator to use words accurately and efficiently. The first sentences in paragraphs do something similar for the busy reader: by avoiding run-on paragraphs you are avoiding the danger of a skim reader failing to notice what is of importance in each of your paragraphs.

You already know (and probably never really think about) when you begin a paragraph. You do it when you come to a substantial new thought, idea or concept, or the next stage in your argument. You then begin a new paragraph with each stage in the development of that thought, idea or argument. When you come to the end of the overall thought, idea or argument you will put in a final paragraph (or section) break for that part of the dissertation or report.

For example, in a document considering the flooding of a property you might decide to consider the rising water table in the area as a cause of the flooding. You might develop a line of argument like this:

It has been suggested that ground water is the cause of flooding for this property ... **a few sentences on when and where this was suggested**.

↓ new paragraph

There has been similar flooding in the adjacent village and ground water was found to be the problem there ... **a few sentences describing the situation in the adjacent village**.

↓ new paragraph

The property is only 1.3 kilometres from the nearest flood plain, but 16 kilometres from the nearest waterway ... **a few sentences stating why these distances make river flooding unlikely in this case**.

↓ new paragraph

The water table was noted as being especially high after recent heavy rainfall ... **a few sentences giving facts and figure about this, reaching the conclusion in the final sentence of the paragraph that this is the main cause of the flooding**.

Having made this series of points you can feel confident that your reader will agree with you and you can move on to your next area for discussion, which will begin with the next new paragraph.

I have suggested that the decision to start a new paragraph usually feels quite natural, so you are unlikely to struggle too much with this. If it is a problem for you, it might be because you did not plan in as much detail as was needed, or you are going off your plan into uncharted territory. If this is the case, you need to go back to the section of your dissertation or report that is written and make sure that you have enough paragraph breaks. Your problem is not likely to be where paragraphs start, but where they should end, so remember the run-on paragraph I offered you earlier in this chapter and guard against any break which does not allow the reader to escape from the document.

If you find this difficult to do, you are probably struggling with what you are trying to say rather than with your ability to paragraph, so you might try putting a brief temporary heading at the beginning of each paragraph: this can help make clear whether you have the right division of text into paragraphs and also whether your argument is flowing well. Although we have been exploring paragraphs because of their importance to the reader, they are valuable to you, too, as the writer. They help to keep you on track and, when used correctly, they help to strengthen the thrust of your argument and increase the impact of your material.

22
Sections and chapters

Dissertations are sometimes divided into chapters, sometimes into sections, and sometimes both are used. Reports are divided using numbered headings which show the importance of the material in each section, moving from a main level heading down to second, third and fourth level headings and so on (this was discussed in detail in the part on planning).

How you divide material will relate directly back to your plan: each section of your plan will represent a main section (or chapter) of your finished document. There is comfort in this: you will not need to worry about structuring as you write, you will be confident in your plan and know in advance where your writing is leading you and the reader. However, even with an effective plan you are still left with two potentially thorny areas: your introduction and your conclusion (or conclusions, as the section is termed in reports).

 **Top Tip**

However settled you feel about the ordering of material in a document as you write it, you might change your mind in the editing and checking stages, or during the review process. For this reason it is usually best to cross-reference lightly where you can, and to give descriptive cross-references where possible (such as my reference to 'the part on planning' in the first paragraph of this chapter). Although this is not always desirable or possible, if you can do it you will be reducing the risk of frustrating your readers when they come to check a page reference that is inaccurate.

Careful introductions

An introduction to a report or a dissertation needs to be carefully crafted and as complete as you can make it. The readers should be left feeling that they are beginning on the journey just as you did; they should feel confident about where you are going and your ability to get there, and reassured about what is being asked of them. It is for this reason that I would not hold with the advice which writers are often given, to write the rest of their document first and then return to write the introduction. There are several ways in which this method can fail you:

- In a lengthy document it can be difficult, by the end, to recall everything you wrote and so your introduction might be lacking if written in this way.
- You might be tempted just to cut and paste sections of your report and then précis them down for the introduction: this usually looks and feels odd to the reader.
- Once you have written the rest of the document it might be difficult for you to produce an introduction which sounds objective: you would not want to seem to be trying to bias the reader too greatly at such an early stage.
- You are in a different place, intellectually and emotionally, once you have written the document, so rather than the readers beginning a journey with you, the writing voice they hear is tired, perhaps even slightly bored.

Having offered you reasons why you might choose not to write the introduction as the last task in producing a document, let me give you a good reason why writing it first can help you. I always use my introduction as a test of how well I have planned my material and thought through my argument. If I cannot write an introduction straight off, as the first piece of writing I do, I know that something is not right with my plan and I return to it straight away to quiz myself on what I intend to achieve in the document.

In producing an introduction at this stage of the process I know that I will not have found the perfect writing voice and I am aware that I will miss out a few points, but by the end of the introduction I will know that I am sure of my material and clear about the way ahead. This allows me to write with confidence and is the best way I know to test that the plan made is the plan that is needed.

Having urged you to consider producing your introduction at the beginning of the writing process, it is worth noting that this will not necessarily work well for every writer, so I would suggest that you try doing it this way and, if it does not work well for you, you still have the option of writing it last.

Writing is an art and so there will always be plenty of advice on offer, some of it contradictory; trying things out for yourself and deciding which piece of advice works best for you is part of your development as a successful writer.

Top Tip

If you take this approach to introductions it is an easy matter, as part of your checking process, to make a note of any material that you come across which you had not at first thought you would include. This will be minimal and can easily be referenced in the introduction at the checking stage.

You may be working from a detailed template or exemplar for a report, or have discussed the detail of your dissertation introduction with a supervisor or mentor, but if you are working from scratch without this help, here is a checklist of areas you might expect to cover in an introduction:

- Who you are, your area of expertise.
- Your understanding of the report/dissertation requirements.
- Your sphere of reference (scope).
- The areas that you will cover.
- What you do *not* intend to include.
- How your argument will develop.
- A hint of your conclusions.

Who you are, your area of expertise: If you are nervous, you are likely to make this part of the introduction too long, but it can be a useful exercise in confidence building. Write down all that you would want to say if you were meeting your readers for the first time, or beginning a presentation aimed at them, and then go back and précis it down to what you think your readers actually need to know.

Your understanding of the report/dissertation requirements: Even though you may have discussed the document in great detail with your supervisor or mentor, or with your boss or client, you still need to outline the intention of the document. This may be no more than a sentence or two, but it will be invaluable to the reader with whom you have never discussed the work.

Your sphere of reference (scope): Giving an overview of the intentions of the document will be of great value to your readers, but it may also set up a whole raft of expectations about what you are likely to achieve in the document. This is where you rein in those expectations by explaining, in general terms, not just the expanse of your coverage of the subject, but also the limitations to that coverage. You might also give reasons for these limitations (the word count, accessibility of material, the budget); you can be clear about these limitations but try not to be too negative about their impact on the document.

Top Tip

In a dissertation you would not usually expect to see a section entitled 'Scope', and you might not see this in a report either if the scope is just one part of the 'Introduction' section, but it is still helpful to think in terms of a scope in your introductory section. Even if the title is not used, you will usually want to include these points.

The areas that you will cover: These might properly be thought of as included in the scope, but it can be useful to see them as slightly separate. The overall scope gives a view of where the document is going; you then need to discuss in more detail the material you will be covering. Again, this need not be a lengthy discussion, but if you were, for example, to be writing a dissertation on Romantic poetry, you might have mentioned that you only have space to write on two poets (scope); you will then go on to explain that you will be discussing the work of Wordsworth and Shelley.

What you do *not* intend to include: This part of your introduction can feel uncomfortable to write. You want to be enthusiastic and assertive, yet you are forcing yourself to focus for a moment on what you might see as a negative aspect of the document. It is, however, easy to turn this around in your mind and see it as positive. You will not want your readers to be even marginally preoccupied by the fact that they are waiting for something that is not going to be covered. In the example I have just given, you would include a brief mention here of the fact that, due to its length and theme, you do not intend to discuss Wordsworth's lengthy autobiographical poem *The Prelude*. Of course, an avid fan of this poem (which is so long that it is published as a book in its own right) might feel a momentary disappointment, but this will pass in moments and is far better than that reader looking out for a reference to it for the entirety of the document.

How your argument will develop: You will not want to get into the detail of your argument here, so this section of the introduction will be a test of your ability to express yourself concisely. You might consider outlining your argument in bullet points so that you do not go off point. Later you could go back and expand each of these into full sentences, knowing that you have captured the essence of your document in a nutshell.

A hint of your conclusions: There is a temptation sometimes to start strongly, so strongly in fact that you appear to be suggesting to your readers that reading the entire document is pointless as they could just take your word for everything in the first few paragraphs. This is a high-risk strategy: you can come across as arrogant or rather bullying, so treat this section with care. You are about to take your readers with you on a journey, and offering a sketch of where you expect to end up with them can be a useful guide for their expectations, but painting the full picture in great detail is likely to make them feel that the pathway for the journey is too rigidly defined.

This might seem like a large amount of material to include in an introduction, but each of these points need only be brief, sometimes just a sentence. This is going to be a challenge, especially as you will be right at the beginning of the writing stage, but you will have plenty of opportunities to come back and polish it up later, so be as bold and as decisive as you can be.

Magnificent conclusions

Conclusions become magnificent when they are brief, complete, assertive, intriguing and reassuring:

Brief: Nobody gets a better grade for a dissertation, or impresses a report reader more, simply because the conclusions section of the document is lengthy. However, many a mark has been lost over a rambling conclusion to a dissertation, and readers will never thank you for a conclusions section to your report which does not give them a clear sense of what you want them to do next.

Complete: You will have offered all of your evidence and rehearsed your argument fully by this stage of the document; all that is required of you now is to bring everything together persuasively, to show the reader that you have both ended up at the same destination. Any new material introduced at this stage will only serve to dissipate that sense of a satisfying conclusion; in a report, it will also show that you are not aware of a strict convention in report writing, stating that no new evidence should be introduced after the main body of the report.

Assertive: By now your readers may be tired; they will certainly be looking forward to the set of conclusions you are about to offer. This puts you in an excellent position as the writer. Your arguments will have been persuasive and your material will have been impressive: an assertive approach now will clinch the support of your readers. To do this, make sure that you only offer firm conclusions (that is, five settled points rather than twenty-five more tentative options) and that you couch them in a positive style of writing (rather than sounding apologetic or uncertain).

Top Tip

For some writers the need to be assertive in this part of a document can become a perennial problem: they seem to lose confidence in themselves right at the end. If you know that you tend to do this, try looking back through your plan just before you write up your conclusions. This can help to ground you in what you are able to achieve. You might also prefer to list all of your conclusions before you write them out in full. That way they will all be in place before you lose your way.

Intriguing: Concluding sections can offer a challenge in this respect. I have urged you to identify your research questions and to use them as the bedrock of your document; I have also suggested that identifying some unanswered research questions to throw out at the end of a document can be appealing. Now I am asking you to also be assertive and reassuring, and you need to fit these requirements against each other. The best way to do this is to make absolutely clear that the research questions you have found along the way were never the target of this document, but might usefully form the basis of a future study. If you are happy with where you are in your journey, this should come through, but I would suggest that you ask a critical friend to read through your concluding section to check that you have not come across as frustrated or indecisive about what you have achieved.

Reassuring: Your readers may be fatigued by now but they will also be enjoying themselves, looking forward to the satisfaction of reaching journey's end with you, agreeing with your conclusions and pondering any new research questions that you have included in this section. Just one suggestion of uncertainty on your part, or one sentence which bemoans your lack of time or resources, or which suggests that you feel disappointed in the outcome of your labours, and you have lost the faith in your work which you have built up over thousands of words. We all of us come to the end of documents with a sense of the path not taken, but you need to end with a pleasing sense of achievement.

Now that we have reached the end of the writing stage of your challenge, you might naturally assume that there is little left to consider, but in fact we are about to embark on one of the most exciting and fulfilling aspects of reports and dissertations: polishing.

PART SIX
Polishing

Polishing your writing is about finding an effective way to check your work so that you can find mistakes and correct them. It is also about much more than this. Polishing will include editing your work so as to make it as impressive as it can be, but also ensuring that it has the greatest possible impact on your reader. This part is therefore concerned with all of the polishing techniques you can employ once you have finished the writing stage, techniques which will be useful to you in a dissertation or report and continue to add impact and style to your writing in the long term.

23

Increasing impact

Impact through your table of contents

It is easy to overlook the impression you might be creating through your table of contents. After all, it has been created as a by-product of all of the other work you have been doing: there is no reason why you would especially have noticed it. However, at this stage you have an ideal opportunity to look at it with a critical eye to see how your reader might view it.

The table of contents is one of the first pages readers will see. It will set the tone for the work and be instrumental in setting up a trusting relationship between the readers and the writer. If the table of contents suggests to readers that you have neglected an area, or that you are being biased, you will instantly incur their suspicions. If, for example, you have developed a pattern of looking in turn at the advantages and then the disadvantages of each aspect of your topic, if you leave out the disadvantages in one aspect, the reader will wonder why. You will have considered the situation and decided that there are none, so reflect this in the table of contents. A heading under which you write a couple of sentences explaining why there are no disadvantages fixes a potentially dangerous situation before it arises.

Whether you are producing a dissertation or a report you will need to include every level of heading in your table of contents. I suggested in the part on planning that, if you are writing a report, you would usually expect to go to a third level of heading. There are, inevitably, plenty of reports which go down beyond this level, but if you are given no exemplars to follow or a style guide suggesting otherwise, this would be a safe level of heading to which you could descend without any concern. You might dip into a fourth level at times, even a fifth for a minor point, but whatever level you use must be recorded in the table of contents. Similarly for a dissertation, if you have a plethora of chapter headings, section headings and more minor headings, include them all. Neither a dissertation nor a report would usually include an index so the table of contents is the only guide your readers have: make it as useful (to you and your readers) as you possibly can.

Impact through structure

A dissertation can vary widely in the structure that is used, and you might be asked to follow a style guide as to structure. It is typically simpler in structure than a report, which might include more headings and is required generally to stick to a fairly rigid format. As with a dissertation, you could expect to be offered a house style for a report, or you might be given a template with which to work. If this is not the case, here are some guidelines as to the sections a reader would expect to see in a report, laid out in the order in which they would usually occur:

1. Title page, which would include:

- title of the report
- date of the report, written unambiguously with the month as a word
- author's name (with company name, if appropriate)
- classification (for example, 'confidential')
- date (reference number and issue number, if appropriate)
- the client's name and company details (if appropriate)
- document history (issue numbers with dates, names of author(s) or editor(s) and notes of changes to the contents)
- authorising signatures
- distribution list (that is, a list of people who are expected to read it)

 **Top Tip**

The title page might be the most impressive page of the report in terms of its visual impact. You might choose to add a company logo or a mission statement to it, or include images or a slick background layout.

2. Acknowledgements

In academic reports these often appear at the end of the report rather than at the beginning, and this is also sometimes the case with professional reports. There is no set form of words to use, although you would not want to be too overly flamboyant in offering your thanks. If you are producing a report for an organisation, you usually do not thank anyone who works for that organisation, acknowledging only external help.

Top Tip

It seems like such a nice thing to do, to acknowledge the help of a supporter or critical friend, but always ask for their permission first. It is not that they would not want to be associated with your report, but they might want to avoid others asking for their help in this area in the future if, for example, they have moved on to other areas of interest.

3. Summaries

Conventions differ as to how a document should be summarised. I will work through with you some general guidance as to the different types of summary and how they might work, always bearing in mind that you would need to follow an organisational style guide if you are asked to do so. You might only include one form of summary, or you might include two or all of those described here.

Abstract or synopsis: The terms are used interchangeably in most cases, although there are those who would fiercely defend one or other of the terms in particular situations. Their use is not limited to reports, which makes the situation even more complicated. A paper at a conference may have an abstract; there may be a synopsis offered at the opening of a journal article. All you need to know here, whichever term you use, is that an abstract or synopsis is designed to help the readers do two things: decide whether to read your report, and gain a sense of where you argument is going to lead them. It is not intended to précis every single point of your report, but rather to give an accurate flavour of the document.

An abstract is often word limited (for example, 200–300 words) and it can be designed for electronic or online keyword searching. With this in mind, you might produce a 'narrative abstract', which outlines your work and which might either include keywords in it or might list them below the body of the abstract. Alternatively, you might produce an abstract which is simply a list of keywords.

Top Tip

Your abstract might appear on the front page of a report or as a separate page. If you think about the types of reader you have and the ways in which they might be using the report, you can then decide on the positioning of your abstract so as to maximise its impact.

Executive summary: This type of summary was originally intended for use by members of the executive of an organisation, allowing them to grasp an overview of your report quickly and effectively. It is therefore, in effect, a gist summary.

Top Tip

The name of this summary sounds rather important and so it has been taken up by some organisations as their main form of report summary, hence the confusion today between the 'executive summary' and the 'summary'.

Summary: A full summary is intended to be a secure means of gaining an entire overview of a report. Your readers should finish reading your summary with confidence that they are missing nothing salient from your report. You will include an introduction and scope, in the briefest possible terms, followed by an overview of the evidence (you will not be able to give much detail about the evidence, but you can indicate its range) and ending with all of your conclusions and recommendations.

Top Tip

You will always be balancing the necessity for brevity in a summary against the need to reassure the reader that it includes all that is required. In a report with many conclusions and a long list of recommendations this can be difficult. If you want to guide the reader and keep it brief, you could include only the most important conclusions and recommendations in the summary and direct the reader to the full report for more minor points. You will always have to make sure that you do direct the reader in this way, though. Readers feel cheated if a conclusion or recommendation comes as a complete surprise in the full report.

4. Table of Contents (often referred to as the TOC)

The minimum expectation here is that you would include the numbers of your heading on the left hand side of the page, followed by the title of the heading and then the page number at which that section begins, on the right hand side of the page. Your word processing package will do this for you automatically once you have set it up for that document, but you might want to consider what else you could include on a table of contents page. It is becoming increasingly popular to add a list of all of your graphs, then all of your tables, figures and so forth at the bottom of your table of contents. Indeed, you can make your table of contents as detailed and extensive as you like, so think at this stage about how the impact of the document could be heightened by your table of contents.

Top Tip

It is the easiest thing in the world to produce a beautifully laid out and accurate table of contents, then change your mind in the polishing stage and add an extra section to your document, forgetting that this now invalidates your table of contents. Always make sure that you update your table of contents right at the end of the polishing stage.

5. Main body

This section will include all of the evidence which you are including to support your argument. Sometimes the introduction is taken as included in the main body and other times it is described as a separate entity. The main body will be numbered sequentially, although some organisations choose not to number the introductory section and only begin to number, using decimal notation, from the section immediately after the introduction.

Top Tip

Although it is probably obvious to you, it should be noted that there is never, ever a section of a report entitled 'main body'. This is the term that is used to describe all of the headings and subheadings you will use to structure your report, rather than a heading in itself.

6. Conclusions

In this section you will be bringing together the arguments you have made and, from the evidence you have offered in the main body, drawing conclusions for the reader. Although it is effectively one topic ('here are my conclusions'), you might choose to divide it into subsections which deal with different aspects of the topic.

7. Recommendations

This seems like an obvious corollary from a conclusions section, and it is, but sometimes it is a little too obvious to make it easy. If you cannot reasonably distinguish between conclusions and recommendations in a way that creates the right kind of impact, you might consider positioning them together in one section entitled 'conclusions and recommendations'.

Top Tip

You have a level of discretion in how the final sections of a report are structured. In scientific reports, for example, you may well not have a 'conclusions' or a 'recommendations' section and instead have a section entitled 'discussion' or similar. It would be very rare to have a 'recommendations' section which was not preceded by conclusions, but it might be appropriate to include a 'conclusions' section as your final section, without following it by a 'recommendations' section.

8. Appendices

These represent the first of two ways in which you might attach material to a report. Appendices are documents on which you can put your own page numbers and they can therefore commence as soon as your report finishes. For example, if the last page of the report is page number 31, Appendix A will be on page 32, Appendix B on pages 32–35, Appendix C on page 36, and so on. For practical purposes, the page numbering would mean that appendices are usually pages which you have created on your computer or which you can copy into your document so that you can paginate them.

You might choose to produce several different series of appendices if you think that this might increase the impact of what you are aiming to do. So, for example, Appendix A through to Appendix F might be a series of small computerised sketches you have created to describe several possible situations and these could be followed by Appendices 1 to 4, your calculations as to the effect of altitude on the situations you are exploring, which could be followed by Appendix I through to VI, covering six potential working solutions, to be read in conjunction with your conclusions. You can also categorise annexes in this way.

Top Tip

The plural of 'appendix' is 'appendices'; in British English the singular of 'annexes' is 'annexe'. If you already knew that you might be wondering why I would stop to make such a minor point. It is because, for those who do not know it, this can cause some confusion and embarrassment.

9. Annexes

This second term for attached material is used for those documents which already have pages numbers on them. These might include a leaflet, a set of maps, another report, a government briefing document. They come after the appendices and are listed in the table of contents but without any mention of their page numbers.

Top Tip

Organisations differ in their approach to appendices and annexes. Occasionally you will find that an organisation will produce all of their reports as text-only documents, putting all of the additional material (graphs, charts, tables and so forth) at the end as either appendices or annexes. Others would prefer to include most of the immediately relevant material in the report itself, leaving the appendices and annexes purely for the inclusion of tangential information and material which is of value to the reader but is too lengthy to place in the report itself. In the latter way, one pertinent graph would be included at the point at which it is being discussed in detail, but the series of six graphs from which the one is taken would be included for general reference in an appendix. Both of these approaches work, although I would argue that the latter generally produces a more easily digested report than the former.

10. References

This can be the most idiosyncratic section of a report. It might include a sub-section entitled 'references', which could refer to documents from which direct quotations have been taken in the report; there might also be a section entitled 'bibliography', which would be, as in a dissertation, a list of texts to which the writer has referred. There might be a 'further reading' section, which could be akin to a recommended reading list for the reader of the report and might include texts which even the writer has not yet read (for example, a government report which has yet to be published but which might be of relevance).

There are occasions when a project timeline might be included in the 'references' section on the basis that it might be of interest to readers of all reports produced during the period of that project, but might not be relevant to any particular part of this report. Tables of weights and measures and international conversion charts might be included on a similar basis: they will not be referenced directly in the report but they might be useful to the reader.

In addition to all of this material (some, all or none of which might be present) there will, if you have used terms with which a reader might be unfamiliar, be a 'glossary'. This gives a list of terms and an explanation of what they mean in the context of the report. If you use any abbreviations in the report you will also include a 'list of abbreviations' and include *every* acronym or initialism you have used with the full term shown beside it.

Top Tip

The placing of a glossary and/or a list of abbreviations makes a difference in a report, even though you might have little choice in the matter if you are following a house style. The easiest position from the readers' point of view is probably at the very end of the report. It is the part of the document to which they might refer most often in reading your report so it makes sense to put it in the most easily accessible place. However, many house style guides give preference to a position nearer the front of the report, often just before or just after the table of contents.

In terms of the impact of your report, the references section is clearly important. If your reader comes across just one quote which is unreferenced, or sees mention of one term with which he or she is unfamiliar, you will have lost much of the positive impact of your writing amidst the negative effect of frustration.

Top Tip

Although I have made a distinction here between a 'glossary' and a 'list of abbreviations', the term 'glossary' is quite wide ranging and there are report writers who would include the list of abbreviations as part of the glossary.

Impact through ordering

We all tend to write as we think at times, and this can result in a disappointing response from our readers. It can also lead to confusion as to how much data to include in the main body of a report and where to place it to greatest effect.

Our natural tendency may be to write in this order:

BACKGROUND

↓

CONTEXT

↓

PROBLEM

↓

SOLUTION

↓

YOUR ROLE

↓

YOUR READER'S RESPONSE

Imagine for a moment that I ask you whether you have sorted out a problem I was having with my computer: this is the order you naturally use to explain that you fixed it for me. You might say:

> These computers are always going wrong (background); it is because of the new security update they put in last year (context) and that led to your internet access being more restricted than before (problem). It just needed the settings altered though (solution) so I did that for you (your role). It might be worth you contacting support services and asking them to alter your settings permanently so that it never happens again (the response you want me to give).

If you reverse this order, your report could become more effective:

YOUR READER'S RESPONSE
(what do you hope to achieve?)

↓

YOUR ROLE
(what have you done?)

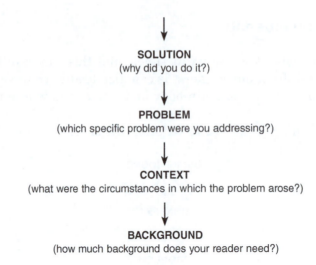

↓

SOLUTION
(why did you do it?)

↓

PROBLEM
(which specific problem were you addressing?)

↓

CONTEXT
(what were the circumstances in which the problem arose?)

↓

BACKGROUND
(how much background does your reader need?)

Of course, you cannot change the ordering of your report sections without causing consternation, but the tension between our natural tendency to 'tell a story' and the reader's need to get an answer is why reports are structured as they are. The impatient or busy reader can cut straight to the conclusions or recommendations section, or can get an overview in the summary prior to reading any detail in the report. Although I am not proposing that you alter the structure of your report, I am recommending that you try to ensure that you mirror the ordering suggested here in some, or all, of the sections of your report. Rather than making your reader wait until the end of the section before really grasping why the section is important, begin the section with this (your reader's response), how it relates to the work you have carried out or to your research (your role) and how it contributes to the aims of the report (the solution). In those sections where it is relevant, you might also include a reminder of the problem (either in this particular section of the report or in the whole document, which would offer both context and background).

This change from our natural tendency in ordering can have an impact beyond reports. You can see it day to day in your emails: how much more effective might you be if you began each email with a clear sense of what you hope to achieve by the email? If you look back now to the last ten emails you sent and/or received and put the last couple of sentences at the beginning of the email, you will be able to see how much difference this could make.

A move away from the traditional to a more targeted ordering in a dissertation can also be very effective. If it is being assessed, your reader response can be assumed (to be impressed, to award a good grade) but you could achieve this more easily by ensuring that, for each section of the dissertation, you begin with material which strengthens the relationship between writer and reader. This could be done by reminding the reader of what has been achieved so far in the work (your role), which might also be joined by a brief recap of the research questions on which you are focusing (problem) and how these are relevant to the overall purpose of the dissertation (context and background). This might take no more than 2–3 sentences at the opening of each chapter/section of your dissertation, but it could significantly increase the impact of your material.

Impact on the page

When you are immersed in the minutiae of your material, focused on your plan and concentrating on what you are aiming to achieve by your writing, it can be difficult to focus on the detail of presentation, especially when it comes to the insertion of graphic material such as graphs, charts, tables, illustrations and so forth. You might have worked hard to source suitable images, or produced them yourself with great care, but you can easily reduce their impact with the way in which they are displayed. Here are some tips:

1. Remember to cite every insertion that was not created by you. Do this beneath the title for the insert by putting the details of your source in brackets.
2. If you are using scanned material from another source, make sure that it is legible and not so cluttered with material irrelevant to your document that it fails to serve your purpose.
3. If you are creating your own insertion, remember to check when you insert it that you have used the same font style and size for each of your insertions. This may be smaller than the font of your main text, which is fine, but you need to use the same size and style of font for each insert unless you have good reason to change it.
4. Label every single insert, or none at all. This sounds basic, I know, but it is easy to forget to do this as you put a document together. You would expect to label inserts unless you are treating them as illustrations which are described fully and unambiguously in the text that surrounds them.
5. Never worry about repetition. You can happily include an insert several times in a document if you judge that the reader needs to see it in several different places. This might be because it is so detailed that it needs to be right in front of the reader each time you write about it. Even though you have included it in your main document, this does not mean that it should not be included in any appendices or annexes you attach to your document. If you think it would make things easier for the reader to have it there too, then include it.
6. Be uniform in the way you present inserted material. If you are using a system, be consistent. So, for example, you might insert 'Figure 1, Figure 2, Figure 3' and so forth. If you then change to 'Figure A', a reader will want to be able to see clearly why you have changed your system. It is usually safer to produce a simple system whereby all figures are numbered sequentially. If you refer to a figure by its specific number, you will give it as a proper noun, which begins with a capital letter ('Figure 8', for example) whereas if you are simply referring to a figure without its specific number, there is no need to capitalise in this way ('as you can see from the figure above', for example).

7. Without necessarily recognising it, readers are always impressed with white space. This gives you the opportunity to increase the impact of your inserted material with very little effort. Leave plenty of clean white space around each insert: it will make the insert and your writing overall look more impressive.

8. If you have been producing material for another purpose recently and the limit was not a word count but a space limit (such as, for example, a journal article or a poster presentation), you might have had to squash your material in response to that limitation. When you come back and write your dissertation or report, remind yourself that such a limitation no longer applies and you can enjoy white space again.

Impact through your language

If you are aiming to create impact through your writing you will want to avoid being either too wordy or too note-like in your writing style. You will want, at times, to adopt a flowing style without becoming rambling and at other times you will want to be succinct without becoming brusque. The way to ensure that you have this level of control over your writing is to analyse it, using a 'power and paste' system.

Each word you produce can be categorised as 'power' (that is, a word which conveys an essential meaning) or 'paste' (a word you could lose without also losing your essential message). Power words are not necessarily (or, indeed, usually) powerful words. Powerful words, such as 'absolutely', 'extremely' and so forth, would only very rarely be considered power words. Paste words might not convey your essential meaning, but they are still valuable in writing as they help our language make sense and, beyond this, they make it flow. The key is to be able to identify the power and paste words in your writing and then to produce writing that has a proportion of each which suits what you are trying to achieve.

Whether a word can be designated as 'power' or 'paste' usually depends on context. The examples below will demonstrate how this works, using the word 'hate', which, at first glance, one might assume was always a power word:

1. Much as I hate to say it, we cannot possibly come to the lunch today and so will have to decline your invitation.
   → here 'hate' is paste; I just want to say 'no' to the lunch invitation.
2. I hate this book.
   → here it has become power; in fact each word in this sentence could be argued to be a power word because it is difficult to see what could be removed without losing the meaning, with the possible exception of 'this'.
3. His was an oppressive, loathed and, indeed, hated regime.
   → 'hated' is paste here on the basis that 'loathed' did the work needed; 'hated' is therefore redundant.

4. Hating your classes is regrettable, but you still have to go to every class.
   → again, 'hating' is paste on the basis that the essential message comes after the comma; what comes before it is just softening the blow. This may add emotionally to the sentence but does not add to its essential meaning.
5. Hatred is the root of all evil.
   → 'hatred' is power, being an inescapable part of the meaning here.
6. I hate to ask you this so soon after my earlier rejection, but is there any possibility, any teeny tiny chance, that you could do me the enormous favour of accepting my willingness to respond to your too kind offer of marriage in the affirmative?
   → way too much paste here! The writer could just have said 'yes'.

Having shown how context dictates whether a word is 'power' or 'paste', we should also recognise that this is an art, not a science. There are always likely to be differences of opinion over the categorisation from time to time. If, in the first example offered here, I was refusing a lunch date with a dear friend for the sixth time in a row, and I knew that she was deeply depressed, and I felt that she no longer believed my reasons for not meeting up, however genuine they were, I might argue that 'much as I hate to say it' is an essential part of my meaning, because I mean to say how terribly sorry I am that I have been unable to make our regular lunch dates recently, and that I hope this will not have a detrimental effect on our friendship.

To give you the chance to try this out, I have written the following paragraph, which contains 184 words, most of which are not being used to convey the essential message.

In the unlikely event, and, in all honesty, it is a highly unlikely event, that there is a general election as soon as in the next three months, it would be more than monstrous to assume that our current political leaders would, yet again, be carried aloft to triumph, there to stalk the corridors of power for another term of office; we need a change of government. Six months would be a more reasonable expectation. Indeed, nine months would be even better for most voters, who have been nagged from pillar to post for decades now about the need to become 'empowered voters', yet the ballot box system, which no doubt worked splendidly in the forum in ancient Rome, is hardly appropriate for our modern day internet age, where online voting should be possible and, surely to goodness, available to all. Another thing which would gall any right-minded citizen at this moment in time is the way in which our politicians assume that an election in five months is a reasonable expectation, which it absolutely is not, in the humble opinion of this writer.

Underline, circle or otherwise identify the words which you believe are power words, the words which convey the essential message being offered by this writer in this paragraph.

The power words in the paragraph are marked here:

In the unlikely event, and, in all honesty, it is a highly unlikely event, that there is a **general election** as soon as **in** the **next three months**, it would be more than monstrous to assume that our current political leaders would, yet again, be carried aloft to triumph, there to stalk the corridors of power for another term of office; **we need** a **change** of **government**. Six months would be a more reasonable expectation. Indeed, **nine months** would be even **better for most voters**, who have been nagged from pillar to post for decades now about the need to become '**empowered voters**', yet the ballot box system, which no doubt worked splendidly in the forum in ancient Rome, is hardly appropriate for our modern day internet age, where **online voting** should be possible and, surely to goodness, **available to all**. Another thing which would gall any right-minded citizen at this moment in time is the way in which our politicians assume that an election in five months is a reasonable expectation, which it absolutely is not, in the humble opinion of this writer.

There are 23 power words selected here and we would need to insert some paste words to make them form a sentence:

If there is a general election in the next three months we need a change of government; nine months might be better for most voters. As 'empowered voters' we need an online voting system, which should be available to all.

Although you might have chosen to include a few words more or less than I did in this example, it demonstrates how wordy we can become almost without realising it and it also shows the effect of writing in a rambling style:

1. The writer takes a long time to get to the subject of the paragraph: the general election.
2. There is increasing confusion over when this is expected to take place: three months is suggested, although nine months is preferred, but then six months is argued as the most likely timing, which makes a nonsense of introducing five months towards the end.
3. We gain a full sense of the personality of the writer at the expense of information and argument.
4. Clichés abound, making this too conversational: 'in all honesty', 'stalk the corridors of power', 'from pillar to post' and 'at this moment in time'.
5. The superlatives and exaggerations make the whole paragraph seem too personal and potentially unreliable: 'highly unlikely', 'more than monstrous', 'carried aloft to power', 'splendidly' and 'absolutely is not'.
6. The last sentence is confusing and irrelevant to the argument the writer is trying to espouse.

Looking back at your experience with this paragraph, did you come to approximately the same number of words? Did you think that the points I had identified were the most important, or did you want to include more points? If you chose far fewer than 23 words you might be too note-like in your style; far more than 23 words and you could have a tendency towards rambling.

The number of words you chose is important, but so too is how easy or difficult you found the process. If you struggled to reduce the word count, or you kept changing your mind, this might be an indication that you have a tendency towards rambling, even if you are usually able to keep it in check. It might come out occasionally in your writing, where you might introduce a hugely long sentence every now and then before reining yourself back in.

It is quite difficult to analyse your own writing in this way, as you will naturally incline towards believing that all of the words and points are of importance, given that you chose to include them in the first place. It is easier to carry out this analysis of your writing with a critical friend. Swap pieces of writing (you will need about 5–6 pages) and mark with highlighter pens on each other's writing the words that you consider to be power words. Although you will not agree entirely, when you swap your work back, take a look and make an instant judgement: is there hardly any highlighter on yours, or does every second word seem to be highlighted? If there is a sea of highlighter, then perhaps it is because the piece of writing was intended to be very succinct, but if this is not the case you will need to work on being more flowing and persuasive in your style. If there is a dearth of highlighter, you might question your ability to come to the point.

Usually, fixing the problem of being too note-like in your writing is no great problem. It is often the result of having to write documents which are very succinct, or perhaps a natural style you picked up at an early stage of your writing. For most writers, seeing this problem highlighted through an exercise such as this is all it takes to trigger a tendency to introduce more words and produce a more discursive style of writing. You will need to do this because writing that is too note-like can come across as aggressive or even arrogant.

For those who are more rambling, the effects can be threefold:

1. It takes time for your reader to reach the crux of what you want to say.
2. The kernel of your point is disguised behind too many words.
3. You might have a tendency to add irrelevancies, especially to the ends of paragraphs.

There are two ways in which you can control any tendency to ramble in your writing style. The first is to carry out this exercise on your own writing regularly (every 6–9 months would work well) so as to keep a check on your style. The second is more time consuming, but you might only need to do it every couple of years. Try producing your entire document as a series of bullet-pointed lists, one for each section of your document. Leave it alone for a day or so, then return to it and question yourself. Do you truly need every single one of those points? If you do, that is fine; if you do not, it is easy to remove the stray points and expand each remaining point out into persuasive English, but without adding any more points back in to the document. This discipline has a remarkable effect on the work of some writers, so it is worth a try if this is a problem for you.

Impact through punctuation

In a language principally composed of words and punctuation marks, it is perhaps unexpected that so many writers choose to abandon one or more pieces of punctuation, but they do. This is sometimes the result of inexpert or harshly offered advice which is not properly explained, so that it seems easier not to use commas at all than to fall into what you have been told is 'your' problem of using too many commas. Sometimes it is the result of a vague and uncomfortable feeling that you have not grasped a punctuation rule fully and so would prefer not to risk getting it wrong.

There are books available which are dedicated entirely to the topic of punctuation and it is not the purpose of this guide to exhaust every punctuation possibility, but I would like to explore with you how you can polish up some of your basic punctuation skills in order to improve your style. As with the other advice in this final section of the book, this is something that you might initially do retrospectively, by examining your writing at the checking stage to see how successful your use of punctuation has been and using this as a spur and guide as you edit your writing and produce your next document.

For the purposes of this guide I would ask you to think of your writing as if it were a road along which your reader is travelling. You have laid down the road, you have told the reader something of the final destination, you have signposted along the way; now you will need punctuation so as to control the nuances of that journey.

A full stop in your writing is like a brick wall in the road. The reader must stop and pause long enough to walk around the brick wall; the reader might also, at this point, take a break from your writing altogether.

Top Tip

Any punctuation mark with a full stop at the bottom of it is referred to as 'hard punctuation', so an exclamation mark and a question mark would both fall into this category. Both of these should be used extremely sparingly in formal writing; there are even style guides which prohibit the use of the exclamation mark in formal writing altogether.

A comma is no more than a speed bump or small ramp in the road. It is the point at which you would take a mental breath or, if you were reading it aloud, you might be inclined to take a physical breath. Some writers produce relatively complicated sentences and so need to use more commas than others. There is no rule about the exact number of commas you should use, nor is there a rigid rule about always using a comma after certain words: the idea of taking a breath as you go over the bump in your road is the best guide you can use for the most part.

Top Tip

Commas either side of a phrase can be used instead of brackets, which are sometimes seen nowadays as rather heavy punctuation. You might write, for example, 'The road ahead, however difficult to travel, must be faced with fortitude'. These commas are inserted where you could as easily use brackets (parentheses), and this leaves you free to employ brackets exclusively for directing the reader to material away from the point at which you are writing '(see Figure 12)', for example, or '(please see Appendix C)', or in using the Harvard referencing system.

A colon is an archway in the road. The reader walks straight through it without pause: the archway simply indicates that something else is happening. So, for example, the writer might be indicating 'I am going to use a list format now, going down the page with numbers or bullet points, but just keep reading', or 'I am going to use someone else's words now in a lengthy quote, but just keep reading'.

Top Tip

Many writers only ever use a colon to introduce a list, but it is a much more versatile tool than that. One way in which it is especially useful in dissertations and reports is that it can replace the dash which you might use to add a little afterthought onto the end of a sentence. A dash can sometimes look too informal in such a formal document, but a colon will do just the same job.

A semi-colon is a gate in your road. It requires the reader to stop long enough to open the gate and walk though. It is not the escape point that a full stop represents, so your reader is trapped in your sentence and must read on, but will pause for long enough to really take in and ponder the first part of your sentence before moving on to the second. A semi-colon is not followed by a capital letter, because it is not hard punctuation, but there is one rule that it must always follow: it must be replaceable by a full stop. That is, both parts of the sentence, on either side of the semi-colon, must stand alone as a sentence.

Top Tip

The semi-colon is one of the strongest persuading tools you have in your writer's tool box. It adds emphasis to what you are trying to say and allows you to create complicated yet persuasive sentences. Look back through this guide and you will find plentiful examples of how it can be used.

Impact through technology

There are several ways in which you can use technology to help increase the impact of your writing. If dyslexia is your challenge, there is a range of specialist software that is designed to help. The internet can be a reference point if you need information quickly (always remembering that much of the content is not peer reviewed). You may work with online brainstorming, or use EndNote or a similar tool to organise your referencing.

The technology I particular want to think about with you here, though, is the grammar check which will be available as part of your word processing package. Some writers who do not feel very confident tend to shy away from grammar check, fearing that it might mislead them; others feel that they should really know these things and so should not need to rely on their computer; still others are concerned that using spellcheck has reduced their spelling ability and so wonder if grammar check would have a similarly detrimental effect over time.

All of these concerns are understandable; however, I would still urge you to use grammar check, but only if you are prepared to shout at your machine: 'I am the human being here, and I know that I am right'. There are three examples that come up repeatedly where grammar check tends to offer a confused reading:

1. 'Fragment (consider revising)': most of the time you can ignore this, but it is still worth checking to make sure that grammar check has not spotted an incomplete sentence that you have missed.
2. You used 'that' and grammar check wonders if you meant ', which': again the answer is 'no' on most occasions. Grammar check cannot always be clear about what you are trying to say.

3. Semi-colons: most of the time, if grammar check prompts you to use a semi-colon, you should insert one. The only time it tends to get confused is if you have created a list, so in that context you are better off making your own decision.

No software system, however sophisticated, is going to be able to discern your intent in all things, or have the delicacy of the human hand in forming elegant and responsive writing. There are undeniable benefits to be gained from allowing grammar check to do its best, as long as you are aware that, with just a little application, a human being could always do better.

24

Checking your document

This is going to be a brief chapter for very good reason. You may find checking a document both boring and unproductive, convinced that you cannot find mistakes. This will probably be because you follow the schoolchild's method of checking: reading the document through, twice, from start to finish. This is, for many writers, the worst possible way to check, because it means that they are checking as writers rather than as readers, reviewing the work in exactly the same order in which they wrote it.

I have already considered with you, in the chapter 'Positive pauses', the value to be derived from alienating yourself from your work so that you can see it as a reader rather than a writer. You can do this by reading it aloud, as I suggested there, and also by leaving it to rest for a while. The longer the time you can leave between writing and checking, within reason, the more likely you are to be able to see errors, so plan some rest time into your writing and planning schedule.

 **Top Tip**

A few lucky people are brilliant at checking documents on their computer screen and never need to worry about printing anything out to check it. Most of us are dreadful at checking this way, so make sure that you are one of the lucky few before you rely on this method.

Although not suggesting that you read it through twice, I would argue that looking through it twice makes sense, but the first run-through should be at some speed, fast enough that, whilst you will be able to spot the odd word or two, you will not be able to read whole sentences. What you are trying to gain here is an overview of the shape and pattern of the work: going through it briskly will allow you to see where it does not seem to flow as well as you had hoped.

In this first read-through you will only be aiming to note a few specific points on the document if you come across them:

1. Have you put all the necessary material in appendices? Are there any densely packed parts of your document where you could usefully make the material more accessible either by removing it to an appendix, or by putting it in a different form, or by deleting or rewriting it?
2. Does the introduction match the main body of the document? If you put some material in as you wrote which you had not intended in your plan, this is the time to make a note to amend your introduction.
3. Is the style consistent throughout? Are all of your headings looking uniform? Has your font size or style changed for any reason? Is the spacing correct throughout?
4. Is everything clearly labelled? Are the labels consistent and legible?
5. Have you included enough 'white space'? Is there any point where you need to make a note to yourself to put in bigger section or chapter breaks, or is there any inserted material around which you forgot to put enough white space?
6. Does it 'dip' towards the end? We all tend to flag in our concentration about two-thirds of the way through things: sentences, paragraphs, sections, chapters and entire documents, so this is the point at which you could slow down slightly and keep a look out for blunders.

Once you have completed this first run-through and made all of the corrections and amendments which result from it, you are ready to move to the final check. This will not be a read-through from start to finish, but rather:

1. Logical ordering? Go to your table of contents and check whether, now that you are making a final check on it, the order of every one of your sections is logical, and that the headings and subheadings you have used accurately reflect the content.
2. Summary inclusive enough? Is it brief enough? If you have any form of summary, it could now become a pleasure to craft into its final form, making sure that every word counts and that nothing has been overlooked.
3. Projection of objectivity? Although you will have put your own style on your document and you will have made all sorts of subjective decisions about the material to be included, the order in which it is presented, the argument you choose to make and the way that you express all of this, you still need your reader to believe that this is a trustworthy document, so now is the time to go back, one last time, to your table of contents. Make sure that your reader will be able to have faith in your ability to produce a document with integrity, based on the sections you have included.

4. Conclusions clear? The most impressive dissertations and reports are those with clear, well-expressed conclusions. You will not want too many for the material you have presented and you may have included some research questions which lead the way forward. If you are not completely happy with your final section, then this is when you need to dig deep and take it apart. Rewrite it as a series of bullet points, remove (or relegate to an appendix) any conclusions which you now see are too speculative or too weak, then rewrite the section with commitment. This is not a pleasant thing to have to do at such a late stage, but it could improve your work significantly.
5. Are there any errors in the detail? Now you can do what you had probably expected to be doing at the outset: read the document through once, from start to finish, looking out for any errors.
6. Tone checked? Whilst you are doing this, imagine having a little 'tone troll' on your shoulder, asking you whether at any point you sound anxious, or tired, or nervous, or pompous or impatient. It is surprising how easily these tones can slip into our writing, and it is only at the polishing stage that we tend to notice them.

This two-stage check seems to be asking you to do an awful lot of hard work, far more than just reading your document through twice, but in reality this can be a quicker way to check than reading it through twice, with all the hesitations that boredom tends to bring to that approach. You will, with this method, be able to see your work, perhaps for the first time, as not only its originator but also as an interested reader. You will get a good sense of how well you have expressed yourself, how much your plan supported your writing and how persuasive you have been. Allow this part of the process to be what it should be: a well-deserved pleasure.

25

Now take your fingers off the keyboard …

This is so much easier said than done. You have invested time and effort into the report or dissertation which now sits in front of you. You have corrected the last of the mistakes you found in your final run-through and you know, intellectually, that this is the best you can make the document. At times during its production you will have longed for it to be over; at other times you will have become so lost in it that you could not imagine it ever ending; you might even, at times, have wondered if you were capable of completing it.

Now, just when you are at the point when it will be over, and you can celebrate its completion, you are in danger of ruining much of your hard work. Writers are often completely oblivious to this danger, and yet it is very real. This is how it goes: you decide that it needs just one more little look before you declare it complete. On rereading it you feel that it might be a good idea to add a little more explanation at the outset (you are making it less accessible) and then, on reflection, you cannot decide whether to include some more material, so you play it safe and take material out of an appendix or your filed notes and put it back in the document (now you are making it turgid) and then you feel that it really needs a much longer set of conclusions (so now you look indecisive).

All of this has been done with the best of intentions, of course: your desperate need, in these closing moments, to make it the best it can possibly be. This is natural enough, but it can lead to dreadful indecision and entirely counterproductive meddling. I was considering offering you some sage words of advice from an admired scholar here in support of my point. I had in mind something about the efficacy of silence, or the wisdom of brevity. Instead, I choose to quote from the famous mime artist Marcel Marceau: 'It's good to shut up sometimes'.

You have not just given time to this work, you have invested emotion in it as well, and the urge to tinker with it can be almost irresistible. You can easily convince yourself that just a few more hours would make it so much better, all the while being dimly aware that, in a strange way, you will miss it. I feel very much the same way now after the journey we have taken together in this book, yet I know that it can now stand alone and I can feel confident, as you will be able to by the time you reach this stage, that it will not be significantly improved by any more polishing. So, we will both be facing the same challenge ... the time has come to take our fingers off the keyboard.

Index